THE

MAFIA

COMMISSION

A History of the Board of Directors of La Cosa Nostra

ANDY PETEPIECE

Tellwell Talent
www.tellwell.ca

ISBN
978-0-2288-0670-7 (Paperback)
978-0-2288-0671-4 (eBook)

Acknowledgement

To Patti

Forever and Always

Introduction

Thanks for looking at and perhaps purchasing this book. It is not a definitive, scholarly treatment of the Mafia Commission. Instead, it is a well-researched summary of the history of the Board of Directors of La Cosa Nostra presented in an informal, comfortable, readable style.

This is not a book that you will pick up and be unable to put down before you are finished. More likely you will find reading a chapter at a time the best method of handling the material. In fact, you may even find yourself nodding off. My buddies say my writing is better than NyQuil for putting them to sleep. (I do need new friends)

As you can see I do not take myself too seriously. However, you may rest assured that my knowledge of La Cosa Nostra is second to none. I have spent more than fifty years studying the Mafia for a variety of reasons. I won't bore you with a list of my accomplishments for they are unimportant.

The researching and organization of this work is my reward. Perhaps, you will get some enjoyment from this book. If so that will be icing on the cake.

Notes

COSA NOSTRA

"Cosa Nostra" is the proper term for the Mafia. In the 1960s, the FBI began using "La Cosa Nostra" and its short form, "LCN." Although technically incorrect, the FBI's label has become standard in their files and in court documents, which are primary source material for me. I will use "La Cosa Nostra" and "LCN" throughout the book.

FAMILY NAMES

In 1963 when famous mob turncoat Joe Valachi was preparing to testify before a Senate Committee, his handlers realized that they would have to have some visual aids to help the Senators and the audience better understand Valachi's information.

They made charts of New York's five Mafia Families and labeled them with the names of their then Bosses; (Joe) Bonanno, (Vito) Genovese, (Tommy) Lucchese, (Carlo) Gambino, and (Joseph) Magliocco.

The first four names are still used today. The Magliocco label was changed not long after the hearings for he had been removed as Boss. Briefly, the label was Profaci, the name of the long-time Boss before Magliocco. Around 1970, when the then leader of the Family, Joe Colombo, became famous, his name came into use and has stuck.

I have used these same 1960s era labels to designate each Family going all the way back to their originations in the early 20th century. Hopefully, this will make it easier to follow their histories.

CAPITILIZATION

Unlike many other mob writers, I like to use capitals on "Family," "Boss," "Underboss," "Consigliere," "Capos," and "Soldiers." There is no real reason for it other than the fact I like the way it looks.

Table Of Contents

APPENDIX B
The formal membership of the Commission from 1958 to 1986

APPENDIX C
The formal membership of the Commission from 1987 to the present.

CHAPTER ONE

The Commission Indictment

THE ANNOUNCEMENT

On February 26, 1985, the US government unsealed a massive indictment against the so-called Board of Directors of the Mafia commonly referred to as "The Commission." It was an attempt to bring down the leadership of the five La Cosa Nostra Families, all based in New York City, in one strike. This move was unprecedented and was the result of countless hours of work by a host of "good guys."

William Webster, head of the FBI, said, "The ruling body of the most powerful organized crime elements in the US... has now been brought to the bar of justice."

The recently appointed (1983) US Attorney for the South District, Rudy Giuliani, commented, "This is a great day for law enforcement, but a bad day, maybe the worst, for the Mafia."

Respected, veteran defense attorney, James LaRossa was not impressed or pretended not to be. "Frankly, it reads more like a movie script than an indictment." LaRossa opined to the gathered hoard of media.

THE DEFENDANTS

Facing charges were the Bosses of four of the five New York Families: Paul "Big Paul" Castellano of the Gambinos, Anthony "Tony Ducks" Corallo of the Luccheses, Philip "Rusty" Rastelli of the Bonannos, and Anthony "Fat Tony" Salerno of the Genovese organization.

Colombo Boss Carmine Persico was missing from the original indictment but was added on June 26, 1985. In August of the same year, Bonanno Boss Phil Rastelli was dropped as a defendant. So too was Castellano, who was whacked out in December 1985.

Other individuals were named. Some were not formal members of the Commission but had sat in on meetings as temporary replacements for the Boss, or in an advisory capacity. In this category were; Gennaro "Gerry Lang" Langella, the Underboss and Acting Boss of the Colombo Family, Aniello "Neil" Dellacroce, the long-time Underboss of the Gambino Family, Salvatore "Tom Mix" Santoro and Christopher "Christie Trick" Furnari, the Underboss and Consigliere respectively, of the Lucchese Family.

Changes happened at this level of defendants as well. Bonanno Consigliere Steve "Stevie Beef" Cannone was added in November but died a month later. Death also took Gambino Underboss Dellacroce off the list when he passed away on December 2, 1985.

Soldier Ralph Scopo of the Colombos would be a key figure in the upcoming trial. He had become a prime target when the FBI learned that he was a serious player in the illegal activities of the "Concrete Club" which controlled the laying of concrete in Manhattan. On November 12, 1985, Bonanno soldier Anthony "Bruno" Indelicato joined the group because of his alleged participation in the July 1979 Commission approved murder of Bonanno Boss Carmine Galante and two Associates.

As always, the feds threw in the "cover our rears" move by including in the indictment, "...others known and unknown..."

To the government, this group of individuals was associated together in the Commission (The Enterprise) which operated around the US and other countries.

THE STRUCTURE OF LA COSA NOSTRA

The indictment went on to describe the now familiar story of the structure of La Cosa Nostra (Mafia) which functioned through Families. Each Family was headed by a Boss, an Underboss, and a Consigliere. (Advisor). At the next level were the Capos and beneath them, the Soldiers and the non-formal members called Associates.

MEMBERS OF THE COMMISSION

A chart showing the history of the Bosses or Acting Bosses of all five New York Families from 1931 to 1986 was also included. It was fairly accurate but failed to list three Bosses of the Bonanno Family from the late sixties and early seventies. (DiGregorio 64-66, Sciacca 66-70, Evola 70-73) This error was of little consequence in these matters.

The indictment also noted, that at different times, there were other Families represented on the Commission and correctly named Buffalo, Chicago, Philadelphia, and Detroit. Unfortunately, the New Jersey Family, better known today as the DeCavalcantes, was included. This was an error of long standing. The feds, in the early days of their understanding of La Cosa Nostra, misinterpreted the intermediary activities of Boss Sam "The Plumber" DeCavalcante, on behalf of the Commission, as meaning he was a member. He was not.

WHAT THE COMMISSION DID

The indictment next explained the purposes of the Commission. The list included; making money in joint ventures with other Families, resolving disputes between Families, formally recognizing new Bosses, approving new members in LCN, controlling relations between LCN and the Sicilian Mafia, establishing rules for LCN members to follow, taking steps to maintain order between Families including the use of murder, and finally creating an atmosphere of fear concerning the Commission to ensure obedience.

THE RICO CHARGES

Note
RICO stands for Racketeer Influenced and Corrupt Organizations Act

All the defendants were charged with RICO CONSPIRACY. In simple terms, it meant the defendants were accused of planning (conspiring) to operate the Commission (The Enterprise in legal terms) by committing at least 2 or more crimes (predicate acts). It is not the committing of these crimes.

Each defendant was also charged with substantive RICO. This meant they were accused of actually operating the Commission (not just planning) by committing at least two or more crimes (predicate acts).

RACKETEERING ACTS

In addition to RICO CONSPIRACY and substantive RICO, all the defendants, except Indelicato, were charged with conspiracy to commit extortion. They also faced 12 counts of extortion or attempted extortion. Finally, they were accused of 6 labor bribery violations. These racketing acts may be broadly grouped into three categories:

THE CONCRETE CLUB:

All the charges (conspiracy to commit extortion, extortion, and labor bribery) involved the "Concrete Club" which was run by the Commission, seven concrete companies, and the Cement and Concrete Workers District Council. (It was controlled by defendant Ralph Scopo)

On concrete contracts over $2 million in New York, only the designated seven companies could bid. But the bidding was rigged so that the "Concrete Club" could control who got which contract. Each company theoretically got their turn at the trough. Ironically there were endless disputes.

For the privilege of being in the "Concrete Club," the winner of each contract had to kick back 2%. This money would then be distributed among the Genovese, Gambino, Colombo, and Lucchese Families, all members of the Commission. (At the time the Bonanno Family was banned from the Commission)

The prosecutors were going to try to prove that fear forced the co-operation of the owners of the concrete companies.

LOANSHARKING:

Only Corallo and Santoro were accused of conspiracy to make extortionate extensions of credit which is commonly referred to as loansharking.

MURDER:

Prosecutors accused Anthony Indelicato of three counts of predicate murder on behalf of the Commission. The victims were Bonanno power Carmine Galante, Capo Leonard Coppola, and a restaurant owner named Giuseppe Turrano.

DOUBLE USE

Any two or more convictions on the racketeering acts listed above could be used to prove a pattern of racketeering (committing crimes) which is necessary to convict a defendant of RICO CONSPIRACY or RICO.

THE MEDIA'S REACTION

The arrests and the announcement of the indictment were big news in all types of media. Major TV networks gave it massive coverage, both on their morning programs and in the evening news. Newspapers across the nation created significant headlines. Here is a sampling from areas known to have mob families.

Leaders of 5 NY crime families indicted.
Pittsburgh Post-Gazette, page 1

Indictments target top of NY mob.
Philadelphia Inquirer, page 1

Five Charged as New York Mob Leaders.
St Louis Post-Dispatch page 1

US strikes at core of Big Apple mob.
Chicago Tribune, page 1

5 reputed bosses held in 'bad day' for NY's Mafia.
Detroit Free Press, page 1

US Indicts 5 Top NY Mafia Chieftains.
Los Angeles Times, page 1

Mafia Rulers Arrested.
Democrat and Chronicle from Rochester, N.Y., page 1

KEY FACTORS

This historic indictment was the result of countless hours of work by policemen, federal agents, prosecutors, and the sacrifices of family members. However, the two key ingredients were two federal laws. Without them, the defendants would never have faced these charges.

OMNIBUS CRIME CONTROL and SAFE STREETS ACT

The 1968 Omnibus Crime Control and Safe Streets act allowed for the use of court-approved bugging and wiretapping. The Commission case was mainly built on these tools.

ORGANIZED CRIME CONTROL ACT

Also of great importance was the 1970 Organized Crime Control Act. It contained the details of the RICO law. (Racketeer Influenced and Corrupt Organizations Act) It was a nuclear bomb hanging over the heads of La Cosa Nostra. For example, if the feds could prove that someone had committed two specific criminal acts while being a member of a continuing criminal enterprise such as a mob Family, or in this case, the Commission, he was liable for much severer penalties than as an individual. It intended to nail the leaders of the Mafia and end the revolving prison door caused by short sentences.

Title Five of this Act contained the details of a federal witness security program commonly referred to as "WITSEC." There was now a formal means to deal with witnesses. They would be protected, provided new identities, relocated elsewhere, and given a subsistence amount of money, for a short time, to help them restart their lives. It wasn't a perfect program, but it was a tremendous improvement over previous thrown together schemes or no protection whatsoever.

Many witnesses who testified in the Commission trial benefited from WITSEC. Included in this list were; Angelo "Big Ange" Lonardo, former

Acting Boss of the Cleveland Family; Joseph Cantalupo, a well-connected Colombo Associate; and Fred DeChristopher, a relative of Colombo Boss Carmine "Junior" Persico.

The stage was now set for the most significant trial in mob history. It would not begin until the fall of 1986, but there was much work to be done before then. One of the challenges for the feds was to provide a history of the Commission. We'll do the same in the next chapter.

CHAPTER TWO

Before The Commission: Part One

Before the advent of a governing Board of Directors, commonly called "The Commission," La Cosa Nostra's final arbitrator was a "Boss of Bosses".

CONFIRMATION OF THE EXISTENCE OF A BOSS OF BOSSES

Nicola Gentile was a Sicilian born gangster who was inducted into La Cosa Nostra in Philadelphia at the young age of 21. He spent many years moving about America, often becoming involved in various internal Mafia disputes. Eventually, he got jammed up on narcotics charges and fled back to Sicily. For some reason, in 1963, he decided to put his version of his life story down on paper. Mafia historians have benefited from his decision to this day.

Gentile wrote, "Between the Heads of various "Borgata" or Families, they select the overall Capo Dei Capi (Boss of Bosses), the King, which is the apex of the Onorata Societa. (La Cosa Nostra)."

Another confirmation comes from Joe Bonanno, a long-time Boss, who had his autobiography published in 1983. Bonanno's book has a brief insight into our discussion. In a passage, Bonanno takes exception to the use of the term, "Boss of all Bosses." He wrote, "This view… is vulgar and superficial." He preferred the term "capo consigliere" which he described as a "head counselor, a chief adviser."

Bonanno wrote that the "capo consigliere" was an informal position. He was chosen because the other Bosses thought he was the most powerful and the most respected.

Bonanno wrote, "A capo consigliere is not an executive or an administrator. He is a figurehead whose influence among other Fathers (Bosses) derives not from the imposition of his will on them but their willing cooperation with him."

On the other hand, Gentile clearly sees the Boss of Bosses as an elected position having high power. The proof of his vision will become clearer later in the chapter.

The writings of Gentile and Bonanno confirm that a top man existed in La Cosa Nostra before 1931. We'll ignore Bonanno's dislike of the term "Boss of all Bosses" and Gentile's use of, "Capo Dei Capi" and settle on "Boss of Bosses" for the remainder of the book.

THE FIRST BOSS OF BOSSES

Giuseppe "The Clutch Hand" Morello
1906 (approximate)-1910

Giuseppe Morello was born in Sicily in 1870 and by the age of 24 was sentenced to six years for counterfeiting. He fled to the United States in late 1892, spending a year in New York City before moving south to Louisiana and then Texas, where he eked out a living in agriculture.

By 1890, Morello had been back in New York for three years, unsuccessfully trying to run a series of small businesses. During this era, the Mafia gangs were on what might be described as subsistence wages compared to the future. It was tough making both a legal and an illegal buck. At this point, Morello turned back to the life of crime he had fled from in Sicily.

In June of 1900, Morello was picked up in an investigation of a counterfeiting gang. Fortunately for Morello, no one ratted him out, and he was released. It now appears that this was when Morello decided to form a band of very close Sicilian confederates with rigid discipline.

Over the next two years, many murders and other crimes thought to be connected to the Morello organization occurred. There were no serious legal consequences for Morello. Fear played a prominent role in these results. However, Morello couldn't control everything.

On April 14, 1903, the body of Benedetto Madonia was found in a barrel on East 11th Street near Avenue D in New York. This event created great interest and is still referred to today. Amazingly, the NYPD solved the case within a couple of days. It turned out that the Secret Service had been conducting surveillance in a counterfeiting case. They had seen Madonia with two of Morello's men.

Morello and some Associates were arrested as material witnesses. It was believed that they had relevant information about the crime. Morello's bail was set at $5,000, which was a considerable sum at the time.

After a four day hearing, Morello and his companions had to be released for lack of evidence. As they left the courtroom, on April 22, 1903, Morello et al. were arrested on a perjury charge for denying they knew the victim.

The coroner then held an inquest into Madonia's death. Basically, all it accomplished was to demonstrate the fear everyone had of Morello and the dreaded Mafia. Once on the stand, many witnesses folded leaving the jury unable to conclude who whacked out Madonia. Morello (and the others) walked.

Morello was represented by an expensive lawyer, as were some of his men. Collections had been solicited in the Italian communities in New York and in other cities on the east coast to pay these high fees. This seems to be a clear indication of the prestige (or fear) that Morello and his Family generated.

Morello's crime Family continued to grow in strength over the next six years. However, there was a glitch in their "legitimate" interests for details exist of the bankruptcy of a busy construction company perhaps caused by a general financial downturn in 1905.

MORELLO FALLS FROM POWER

The law came calling again on November 15, 1909, when Morello (and others) were arrested on counterfeiting charges. In February of the next year, Morello was convicted and not long afterward, was hit with 15 and 10-year sentences. By all press accounts at the time, Morello didn't take it very well. Appeals would follow but to no avail.

Note:
We'll pick up the Morello story later in this chapter.

PROOF THAT MORELLO WAS BOSS OF BOSSES

The confirmation that Morello held this position comes from Gentile who wrote, "...Piddu Morello, who had been the Capo Dei Capi of the Onorata Societa since... my induction."

We know Gentile was born in 1885 and he wrote that he was inducted at the age of 21. Doing the math, this meant Gentile formally joined La Cosa Nostra in 1906; thus Morello was Boss of Boss from at least this date till his conviction in 1910.

Note:
Morello was often referred to as "The Clutch Hand" due to the fact he only had the small finger on his right hand. In his later years, he acquired the name "Peter" for some reason.

THE SECOND BOSS OF BOSSES

Salvatore "Toto" D'Aquila
1910-1928

Salvatore "Toto" D'Aquila," the second Boss of Bosses, was born in Palermo, Sicily in November of 1877. He arrived in the USA in 1906. Within five years, he was elected head of La Cosa Nostra. This seems to have been an incredibly fast rise, but there is little source evidence to explain it. Some claim he hooked up with the powerful Morello Family and broke off to form his own organization when Morello went to the slammer in 1910. That explanation seems shaky for why would the other Mafia Bosses, from around the country, elect a Boss of Bosses who had hardly any experience as a Family leader?

It seems more reasonable to assume that, by 1910, D'Aquila had at least two or more years under his belt as Boss of his own Family.

Unfortunately, there is no source evidence to support that theory. Like so many aspects of La Cosa Nostra, the origins of his power will remain elusive.

D'Aquila was married in 1912 and eventually had five children. Various reports listed his legitimate enterprises as being in real estate and importing cheese and olive oil.

PROOF THAT D'AQUILA WAS BOSS OF BOSSES

Gentile clearly states that D'Aquila headed La Cosa Nostra, "his (Morello's) position had been entrusted by the general assembly to Toto D'Aquila."

Bonanno supports this evidence. He wrote, "Among the men who occupied this informal position... were Tata D'Aquila of New York..."

Note:
The General Assembly was a gathering of all the Mafia Bosses in the US.

CONFLICT WITH THE MORELLOS et al

Being voted Boss of Bosses didn't mean that the person sat back and counted the bales of money rolling in. Having power generated cash but holding on to the control was the problem. D'Aquila seemed to be endlessly involved in conspiracies and violence. While it is not sure, it appears that the hits listed below were part of the struggle for power between the D'Aquila Family and the remnants of the Morello organization.

November 4/1913
Joseph Fontana was killed. A source told the Secret Service that Fontana was a member of the D'Aquila Family. Others said he was initially a Morello member. It was alleged that Fontana was killed by an alliance of the Alfred Mineo crew and the Morellos. Mineo was a D'Aquila underling who would later betray his Boss.

November 1913
Giuseppe Fanaro was murdered. He too was thought to be a member of the D'Aquila Family. D'Aquila started striking back at those who were challenging him.

May 23/14
Fortunato "Charles" Lamonti was killed at 108th and 2nd Ave. in New York. He had been named the leader of the Family by Morello upon his incarceration.

This hit was thought to be a counter strike by the D'Aquila forces, but that can't be proven. A source explained to the good guys that the Morellos were unsure who whacked their leader. One thing was sure---Charles Lamonti was dead.

October 13/15
Tomaso "Joe" Lamonti was gunned down at 116th and 1st Ave. He was a brother of the murdered Charles La Monte. The shooter, Antonio Impoluzzo, was caught, convicted, and executed. He

did not reveal who hired him to do the hit. It appears that these murders improved D'Aquila's position in lower Manhattan.

During the next half decade, D'Aquila benefited from a protracted conflict between the Morello Family and a group of Neapolitan gangsters often referred to as the Camorra. The battle was over control of Harlem, and the end result was the decimation of the power of the Camorra groups in New York.

Gentile wrote that as the 1920s began, D'Aquila had exercised his power, convincing the General Assembly to condemn 11 members to death. Included in this group were former Boss of Bosses Giuseppe Morello and Umberto Valenti, a one-time favorite hitman of D'Aquila. In his book, Gentile gave a long, one-sided account of his attempts to save these souls from their death sentences.

From Gentile's prejudiced account we are told that "D'Aquila was a very authoritative figure and that meant that those who didn't support him were condemned to death." Gentile went on to describe how he learned of the "…the wickedness and snares of Toto D'Aquila." The Boss of Bosses had a "ferocious personality," claimed Gentile and was, "worshipped… like a God" by the Boss of Cleveland, Joe Lonardo.

CONFLICT WITH JOE MASSERIA et al

Eventually, Umberto Valenti was lured back into the D'Aquila fold. Valenti was told that the sentence of death would be lifted if he would whack out D'Aquila's chief rival, Giuseppe "Joe the Boss" Masseria. The latter headed his own Family, which included members of the Morello organization. Valenti took on the job. Below are brief descriptions of some of the action. It's not pretty.

May 8/22
Vincent Morello was killed at 116th and 2nd Ave. He was shot from an automobile full of Valenti guys. Vincent Morello had been in the Masseria milieu.

On the same day:
A big gunfight erupted on Grand Street, as Masseria retaliated for the shootings earlier in the day. A child, a woman, and four men were wounded. Later, Frederico Petruzziello (35) was brought to the hospital severely injured. Silvio Tagliogambe was also rushed

in but died. The cops chased and arrested Joe Masseria, as one of the shooters. He threw away a .32 automatic, which was quickly found. Later, Masseria was released on $15,000 bail. Nothing came of the charges.

August 8/22
Joe Masseria was ambushed, as he left his home at 80 Second Ave. Two men crossed the street and tried to kill him. In front of Helney Brother's, a woman's wear store at 82 Second Ave., Masseria dodged three bullets. Two of the slugs hit the window of Helney Brothers.

The two gunmen ran to a waiting car and headed up Fifth Street. They were accosted by a group of men who were manning a nearby picket line. Some picketers ran into the street to try to stop the shooters, but they were fired upon. Six were hit, and one died later in hospital. The police took Masseria in for questioning but learned nothing. This was apparently a D'Aquila strike.

August 11/22
Umberto Valenti was shot at 11:45 AM at the corner of 12th Street and 2nd Ave. after attending a peace meeting in a spaghetti restaurant. Fifteen or twenty shots were fired as he emerged from the eatery. The New York Times described him as "a notorious gunman and bootlegger. An eight-year-old girl and a street cleaner were also hit. The ambushed Valenti died at St Marks Hospital at 12:46 PM. This was a successful hit by the Masseria group.

According to Gentile, D'Aquila, the Boss of Bosses, ordered all his members to avoid the wake and funeral of Valenti. This is a slight usually reserved for someone in disfavor, and apparently, D'Aquila continued to feel this way towards Valenti for he never succeeded in killing Masseria.

DEMONSTRATING HIS POWER

Gentile wrote of a 1923 internal conflict within the Pueblo, Colorado Family. Without the approval of their superiors, a crew began robbing various establishments. Eventually, one of the renegades was whacked out, and three of the group fled to Kansas City. At this time, Gentile was located there and took the three men under his protection. He achieved this by having them transferred into the Kansas City Family, which prevented any other Family from harming them.

Meanwhile, this conflict was reported to D'Aquila, and a meeting of the General Assembly was called. The charges were outlined, and the Bosses then held a vote. According to Gentile, D'Aquila spoke first and called for the death penalty for all three men. The other leaders, taking their cue from the Boss of Bosses, fell into line with their votes.

Gentile claimed he was brave enough to questions the validity of the evidence against the accused. This greatly stunned the other leaders. Eventually, the meeting was adjourned. Later, D'Aquila's Underboss, Joe Traina, tried to frighten Gentile into ending his opposition to D'Aquila's decision. In the end, the three men were expelled from La Cosa Nostra, but their lives were saved. Gentile hadn't improved his relationship with the most powerful man in the Mafia.

D'AQUILA DIES

After being Boss of Bosses for 18 years, D'Aquila had accumulated a long list of enemies and/or those who envied his Family throne. It was inevitable that his end would come.

On October 10, 1928, D'Aquila, his wife, and four children, drove from their Bronx home to the offices of Dr. Cascio at 211 Avenue A in Manhattan. This had become a regular routine for D'Aquila and his wife, who were both reportedly suffering from heart problems. On this day, D'Aquila ended up puttering with the engine of his automobile, while his wife was still inside the doctor's home. It was a fatal decision, as was his practice of being at the same place at the same time for many days. According to witnesses, three men approached D'Aquila, and an argument ensued. More likely the shooters just yelled some insults at the Boss of Bosses as they gunned him down.

D'Aquila was taken out in a plot hatched by his underboss Al Mineo and supported by a crucial rival, Joe Masseria.

THE KING WAS DEAD. LONG LIVE THE KING.

CHAPTER THREE

Before The Commission: Part Two

THE THIRD BOSS OF BOSSES

Giuseppe "Joe the Boss" Masseria
1928-1930

Without question, Giuseppe "Joe the Boss" Masseria is the best known of the four Boss of Bosses. He was born in Sicily on January 17, 1886, and moved to the United States in 1902. From source material, we know he bounced around doing low-level crime work such as a robbery and burglary. The best evidence is that prohibition provided him the opportunity to grow his own organization in lower Manhattan.

The Masseria Family was to be entirely different than the other Families composed mainly of Sicilians. Masseria formed alliances with a group of Neopolitan hoods headed by Vito Genovese. Al Capone, another Neopolitan, eventually became a Capo in the Masseria Family. The group also included a Calabrian gang in Brooklyn controlled by Frankie Yale. Other vital recruits were from the Morello Family. A number of them were under sentences of death from D'Aquila, so they were looking for a safe harbor. The former Boss of Bosses, Giuseppe Morello, was given the rank of Underboss. The net result was that Masseria and his Family were powerful.

In the D'Aquila outline above, we described some hit attempts on Masseria, all of which he survived. In contrast, D'Aquila was not lucky. He was whacked out on October of 1928. This was not the beginning of peace, but just the prelude for an era of even more killings and political intrigue.

PROOF THAT MASSERIA WAS BOSS OF BOSSES

A quote from the Gentile book confirms Masseria's lofty positions. Gentile wrote, "...then he (Masseria) became the Capo Dei Capo..."

Obviously, Masseria was voted into power by a gathering of the General Assembly, late in 1928, but we have no source material on that meeting. Nevertheless, we can date his reign, in this position, from 1928 to 1930. Some will take exception to the closing date, for Masseria didn't die till 1931. The reasoning behind using 1930 will be explained below.

ENDLESS INTRIGUE AND VIOLENCE

Al Capone now enters the story. He was associated with the Masseria group in New York before his brief sojourn as a legitimate man in Baltimore. Early in 1921, Capone was in Chicago. Bonanno wrote, "...it can be assumed that Capone's relocation to Chicago had the blessing of 'Joe the Boss'. Later events would strongly support this statement.

At this point, we'll outline the leadership of the five New York Families so that the reader will have a clearer picture of the various shifting alliances, which were essential factors in the violence that consumed the Masseria era.

Masseria headed up what we now call the Genovese Family, which emerged from the Morello/Masseria organizations. A man named Nicola "Cola" Shiro was Boss of Bonanno Family. Joe Profaci had quietly emerged as the head man of what we now refer to as the Colombo Family. Manfredi "Al" Mineo had replaced D'Aquila as Boss the Gambino Family. The fifth Boss was Gaetano "Tommy" Reina of Lucchese Family.

Note:

The Family names; Genovese, Bonanno, Colombo, Gambino, and Lucchese will be used from this point on in an attempt to avoid confusion and to provide continuity. These labels didn't come into use till the 1960's.

Events began to unfold fast and furiously starting in 1928. To avoid getting bogged down in names and dates, we'll restrict the outline to the significant actions.

Note:
Giuseppe "The Clutch Hand" Morello had been released from prison in 1920. Not long afterward, he reappeared as Underboss to Joe Masseria. At this point, he was often referred to as "Peter" Morello.

July 1, 1928
Masseria Capo, Frankie Yale was gunned down in his vehicle. The machine gun used was linked to Capone, strongly suggesting that Masseria had approved this hit.

September 27, 1928
Anthony Lombardo, Boss of a Sicilian Mafia Family in Chicago, was murdered. Gentile wrote that it was done by Capone's men, at the suggestion of Masseria.

At this point, Gentile claimed that Masseria formally made Capone a member of his Family and appointed him a Capo. This meant Capone would continue to send tribute to Masseria.

October 10, 1928
Boss of Bosses Salvatore "Toto" D'Aquila, was killed in a coup supported by Masseria.

Late in 1928
The General Assembly of La Cosa Nostra elected Masseria as Boss of Bosses

Spring 1929
Joe Bonanno claimed that Masseria visited Joe Aiello in Chicago. (Aiello had replaced Anthony Lombardo as Boss of that city's Mafia Family) Masseria wanted Aiello to make a deal to split up Chicago. Aiello, furious at Masseria's support of Aiello's rival Capone, angrily refused Masseria's offer.

Early 1930

Masseria ordered Detroit Boss Gaspar Milazzo and Buffalo Boss Stefano Magaddino, to New York, to pledge their loyalty and to promise they would not support Chicago Boss Joe Aiello. Both refused the invitation, which infuriated Masseria. A significant mob war was the result.

CASTELLAMMARESE WAR

The conflict was given this label long after the events. Many of those involved had their roots in the Sicilian town of Castellammare del Golfo and thus the name. What follows are brief summaries of some of the significant incidents before the General Assembly tried to find a road to peace.

February 26, 1930

Tommy Reina, Boss of the Lucchese Family, was gunned down in a coup backed by Masseria. Joe Pinzolo, a Masseria puppet, was installed as the new Boss.

May 31, 1930

Detroit Boss Gaspar Milazzo was murdered in a coup supported by Masseria. He was still angry at Milazzo's support of Chicago's Aiello.

June 1930, approximately

Nicola "Cola "Shiro, the Boss of the Bonanno Family, was leery of becoming involved in a mob war. Upon demand, he paid Masseria a $10,000 tribute and went into hiding. The Family elected Salvatore Maranzano as their new Boss. He spearheaded the war against Masseria.

July 1930

Cleveland Boss Joe Porello was murdered along with his brother. He had been supported by Masseria in the past, but this didn't save him.

August 15, 1930
Giuseppe or Peter "Clutch Hand" Morello, Masseria's Underboss and chief strategist, was shot down in his office in New York by Maranzano supporters.

September 9, 1930
Joseph Pinzolo, Masseria's puppet leader of the Lucchese Family, was whacked out, in his office, by men supported by rivals within the Family.

October 30, 1930
Joe Aiello, Boss of the Chicago Mafia Family, was filled full of lead. Capone was behind the hit.

November 5, 1930
Al Mineo, Boss of the Gambino Family, and his Underboss Steve Ferrigno, both Masseria supporters, were ambushed and killed.

PANIC

Things were going downhill fast for Masseria. Also, the New York police were pressuring him to bring the hostilities to an end. Masseria began looking for a way out. His official reign as Boss of Bosses was over.

THE FOURTH BOSS OF BOSSES

Gaspar Messina
Late 1930-1931

By December of 1930, everyone was frightened by the incredible confusion and violence taking place in what we now call "the Castellammarese War."

PROOF THAT MESSINA WAS BOSS OF BOSSES

A General Assembly was held in Boston. According to Gentile, "Around that time, Gaspare Messina was elected provisional Capo dei Capi". Bonanno also supports this assertion although he didn't use the word "provisional" when mentioning Messina being a Boss of Bosses.

Gentile went on to explain that this action had taken place because the General Assembly was going to examine the actions of the sitting Boss of Bosses, Joe Masseria.

The Assembly appointed a commission (delegation) headed by Giuseppe Traina. The one-time Underboss to Salvatore D'Aquila was to meet with Maranzano to see if an end to the conflict could be negotiated. After some difficulty, the committee did sit down with Maranzano but was then subjected to a long-winded explanation of his grievances and justifications for his actions. It was apparently an attempt to win the delegation over to his side rather than a search for grounds for peace.

Another General Assembly was called at which Maranzano dominated. It was clear that he was in no mood for a compromise. He wanted Masseria dead, with everyone falling in line behind himself. Maranzano was probably too vain to realize it, but his autocratic style, on public display, was sowing the seeds for his own destruction.

MASSERIA IS WHACKED

Things hadn't been going well for Masseria, and he was apparently worried. He put his faith in the General Assembly, hoping they could forge peace with Maranzano. Meanwhile, he was keeping the leashes on his own men, so that they didn't disrupt the negotiations. The significant Capos were not pleased.

Gentile reported that Capone met with Lucky Luciano, a rising power in the Masseria Family, and others. They concluded that the only way to obtain peace with Maranzano and go back to business was to whack out their Boss.

Bonanno confirms this plot when he writes that Luciano met with Maranzano, in the spring of 1931, and it was agreed that Luciano would kill Masseria to achieve peace.

On April 15, 1931, Masseria was in the Nuova Villa Tammaro restaurant on Coney Island. He was playing cards with a few other men. Suddenly, two gunmen entered the eatery and opened up on "Joe the Boss" with their revolvers. Five slugs to the back and one to the head ended his life quickly. Rather meanly, Joe Bonanno wrote, "He died on a full stomach, and that leads me to believe he died happy."

THE KING IS DEAD. LONG LIVE THE KING.

THE LAST BOSS OF BOSSES

Salvatore Maranzano
1931-1931

Salvatore Maranzano was born in Sicily on July 31, 1886. He had many connections there and had a reputation of being a fearless warrior. Maranzano ran a successful business in Palermo and seemed set for life. However, he immigrated to the United States in 1925, probably fleeing police pressure back at home.

His transfer into the Nicola "Cola" Shiro (Bonanno Family) organization was quickly arranged and welcomed by all. Soon, Maranzano was running an export/import business, investing in real estate, and operating a mini-empire of stills.

Joe Bonanno was enthralled by Maranzano and rhapsodized about his style in clothing, "He dressed like a conservative businessman," his masterful voice, "...ah, his voice... he had a sweet voice," and his command of men, "He could make everyone in the room think he was talking to them individually."

Gentile, who had met Maranzano a few times, was not impressed. "He graced us like a king," Gentile wrote sarcastically. He went on to describe a meeting and said that "He was furious and resembles a demon."

PROOF THAT MARANZANO WAS BOSS OF BOSSES

After the slaying of Masseria, Joe Bonanno described a series of gatherings at which people recognized Maranzano's power. The main one was held in late May 1931, in Chicago. "Once all the major leaders (Bosses) had been recognized and confirmed by the congregation, the gathered leaders had their turn to show their respect for Maranzano," wrote Bonanno. What he was really saying was that Maranzano was voted Boss of Bosses.

Gentile wrote, "Maranzano was elected Capo dei Capi of the Mafia of the United States."

FAST AND FURIOUS

Maranzano was an autocratic despot, whose ambitions and paranoia knew few bounds. A huge banquet was held in Brooklyn, supposedly to raise money for all those associates who had sacrificed so much in the conflicts. Bonanno spoke of a figure of $80,000, whereas Gentile pegged the take as $100,000. In today's dollars, that would translate into the approximate values of $1.2 million to $1.5 million. That's not chump change!

It turned out Maranzano did not distribute the contributions, which caused concern. Bonanno described the reaction by writing, "Gaspar (DiGregorio) for one, grumbled about Maranzano's tardiness in rewarding us for his war service." Gentile provided an explanation when he said that "Maranzano had prepared a list of 60... Picciotti (members) who had to die."

Soon, other Bosses began planning a coup, for they feared for their lives and the growing power of Maranzano.

According to Gentile, the straw that broke the camel's back was when Maranzano ordered Frank Scalise, Boss of the Gambino Family, to whack out an influential member of his Family. Scalise kept stalling, which infuriated Maranzano. Scalise started fearing for his life, and he had been considered a strong supporter of Maranzano.

Joe Valachi, the famous Mafia turncoat from the early 1960's, confirmed that Maranzano had targeted many other mob powers after Masseria went down. Valachi said, "He (Maranzano) talked about some others who had to go (be killed) like Al Capone, Frank Costello, Willie Moretti..."

Capone joined the plotting of Lucky Luciano and others. The decision was made to whack out the Boss of Bosses. Maranzano would be a challenging target, for he was usually surrounded by bodyguards in an office in a high rise tower in Manhattan. However, for every problem, there is a solution, and that was no different in this case.

Luciano had long associated himself with Jewish gangsters including Meyer Lansky. It was decided that a group of them would pose as tax agents and visit the offices of Maranzano. They would kill him there. The problem was that these hoods didn't know what Maranzano looked like and thus needed someone to finger him.

Some accounts indicate that this job was done by Tommy Lucchese, a future Boss of the Family that took on his name. I think it is more logical to conclude that it was Joe Bonanno who played this role.

Gentile describes how the Jewish mobsters went to Maranzano's office and, "...identified themselves as Federal Agents." The Maranzano men were lined up against the wall. At this point, one of the intruders went out into the hall and brought in an Italian who had been brought along to identify

Maranzano. The Bosses of Bosses looked at the Italian and said, "Peppino, you know I am Maranzano..." Maranzano was still under the impression that these were real government men.

Maranzano was taken into his private office, where the attackers tried to kill him quietly with a knife. The Boss of Bosses put up a tremendous fight, and they had to unload their pistols into him.

THE PROOF THAT BONANNO WAS IN ON THE COUP

The nickname "Peppino" was one used to refer to Bonanno for decades. In the hit, a "Peppino" fingered Maranzano. Bonanno was very close to Maranzano and thus would not misidentify him. Also, Bonanno had much to gain by helping kill his leader. He would become the next Boss. Finally, it was typical for ambitious underlings, to plan a coup, but to also seek support from at least one other powerful Boss. It's not definite, but I am convinced Bonanno was in on the killing of Maranzano.

THE KING IS DEAD. LONG LIVE THE KING. NOT!

CHAPTER FOUR

Forming The Commission

Boss of Bosses Salvatore Maranzano was whacked out on September 10, 1931. Typically, this would call for the election of a new overall leader. At this time, however, the mob Bosses were totally fed up with all the chaos and danger to themselves under the Boss of Bosses system. There had to be a better way.

FIRST ATTEMPT

After the murder of Joe Masseria in April of 1931, a General Assembly was held in Chicago. Gentile recalled that "Some Rappresenti (Bosses), remembering the past dictatorial regime of Masseria, Manfre (Manfredi) and Fanuzzo (Ferrigno), had proposed to elect to the office of Cap dei Capi, a commission composed of six elements (members)"

Maranzano, apparently wanting to be the top dog, countered this move by creating an inquiry body to investigate some alleged misdeeds of the proposed head of this new "Commission" idea. As you can imagine, the Maranzano flunkies dug up enough dirt to put an end to this attempt to bring democracy to the top of the La Cosa Nostra empire.

SECOND ATTEMPT

After the murder of Maranzano, yet another General Assembly was called in Chicago. It was hosted by Capone. From this point on the gathering will be labeled a "National Meeting" of La Cosa Nostra. (It's the term Joe Bonanno used)

Bonanno explained that "We (La Cosa Nostra) replaced leadership by one man with leadership by committee. This group came to be known as the Commission."

Gentile wrote, "…this time it was decided to replace the Capo dei Capi of the Mafia with a Commission of six people, the office would no longer be vested in one person alone." Gentile was mistaken in using the number six. It was probably a typographical error for he later lists seven members. Interestingly Gentile takes credit for the idea of forming the Commission.

THE ORIGINAL MEMBERS OF THE COMMISSION

Bonanno named the seven original Commission members as; Lucky Luciano (Genovese), Tom Gagliano (Lucchese), Joe Profaci (Colombo), Joe Bonanno (Bonanno), Vincent Mangano (Gambino), Stefano Magaddino (Magaddino) and Capone (Chicago).

Gentile listed six of the same names but had Cleveland's Frank Milano as a member and not Buffalo's Stefano Magaddino. His memory was faulty in this instance.

Seven men were chosen for membership. It was to avoid the chance of a tie vote which could happen if there were six, eight, twelve, or any even number of members.

WHY THESE SEVEN MEN WERE CHOSEN

The Bosses of the five New York Families had to sit on the Commission. It was the only mob city to have more than one Family and history had shown that this was where most of the inter-Family disputes took place.

Chicago was seated because Capone and his organization could not be ignored. They were just too powerful. Ironically, it turned out that the Chicago Family rarely was involved in Commission politics.

Why Buffalo? That is an excellent question especially coming from the perspective of today when you'd need a microscope to see any remnants of a Mafia organization in that area. However, in 1931, the Boss of Buffalo,

Stefano Magaddino, was very influential and highly respected. Besides, he was related to Joe Bonanno of New York. It was impossible not to give him a seat at the table.

PROFILES OF THE ORIGINAL COMMISSION MEMBERS

CHARLES "LUCKY" LUCIANO

Luciano is probably American's second best-known gangster, next to Al Capone. He was born in Sicily on November 24, 1897, and moved to New York with his family in 1907. Before long, he was out of school and hustling on the streets with fellows of a like mind.

When Prohibition came in 1920, Lucky joined in the gold rush by associating with pals Frank Costello, Vito Genovese, and Meyer Lansky. With financial backing from the legendary Arnold Rothstein and their connection to Boss Joe Masseria, the group was well placed and piling up the money.

There is little evidence of Luciano being an active participant in the violence between 1930 and 1931. It is likely that he was in on some of the strategizing, but that roll was first trusted to Peter Morello by Masseria. Al Mineo took over after Morello was killed.

The best guess is that as these advisors were taken out, Masseria was forced to turn more closely to Luciano for support. It is clear from both Bonanno, Gentile, and Valachi that as 1931 began, Luciano was a significant figure who had to be dealt with.

By Bonanno's account, Luciano forged an agreement with Maranzano that peace was possible if Masseria was no longer around. Valachi stated that Luciano was present when Joe the Boss was killed, but there is no other reliable evidence to confirm this. As for the often repeated story that, after the murder, Luciano told the police that he was in the washroom relieving himself when the shooting started, no one has been able to find any trace of this statement in police reports. For our purposes, all these details are unimportant.

There is clear evidence, from Bonanno and Gentile, that Luciano and friends were responsible for taking out the autocratic Salvatore Maranzano in the fall of 1931. Luciano was now at the height of his power.

Decades later, Bonanno gave his impression of Luciano which was mostly favorable with some reservations. Bonanno found Luciano to be "avant-garde" as opposed to "old-fashioned." He said Luciano, "Comported himself as a man of respect." But Bonanno was troubled with Luciano's focus on making money rather than paying homage to the "Traditions" held so dear by Bonanno. Bonanno was also concerned about Lucky including non-Sicilians in his entourage. Finally, Bonanno wrote that Luciano considered the possibility of whacking out prosecutor Thomas Dewey, an action Bonanno claimed to be totally against his "Tradition."

This is not the place to give a detailed account of Luciano's life but to focus on some of the more critical events. Clearly, Luciano's controversial conviction, for being involved in prostitution, was a mega-event. On June 18, 1936, Luciano received the stunning sentence of 30-50 years. At that moment, his power began to slowly but surely dissipate.

Countless appeals followed, but Luciano remained in prison. The future looked grim. Then events began turning his way again. The United States joined World War Two in December of 1941. Suddenly the safety of the eastern seaboard docks, critical for the movement of supplies to Europe, was a high priority. An accidental fire resulted in the sinking of a large cruise ship, the Normandie that was being converted into a troop carrier. This convinced Naval Intelligence that they had to protect the docks at all costs.

Knowing that the Italian mob controlled the dock workers through unions, the Navy came knocking and eventually ended up talking with Luciano. He passed the word for the leaders on the docks to co-operate with the Navy. Luciano also ordered his flunkies to encourage Sicilian immigrants to share their memories and pictures of Sicily with the Navy, as Sicily was a possible target of invasion by the allies.

In February of 1946, Luciano won a recommendation of release from his parole board. They were convinced he had made a contribution to the war effort. They were uncertain of the value of his work, but it was enough. Once the parole board had made their decision, Governor Thomas Dewey signed the final papers. Luciano was free.

Lucky was taken to Ellis Island to await deportation. On February 10, 1946, the forlorn Luciano was put on the freighter S.S. Laure Keene which began its journey to Italy. For all intents and purposes, his power was now completely gone.

Later that year, Lucky began a long-shot attempt to regain some of his power. He quietly, legally, entered Cuba, on October 29, on a 60-day visa. Unfortunately for him, in February of 1947, media accounts of his presence in Cuba reached the eyes of American officials. Pressure was put on the Cuban government, which resulted in Luciano being deported on March 20, 1947. It was all downhill from there.

For the next 16 years, Luciano languished in Italy making some failed attempts at running a legitimate business. At first, he received a decent amount of cash from his friends in America, but as time passed, these envelopes grew smaller and smaller. By the early 1960s, he was so broke that he seriously contemplated having his biography written and perhaps a movie made. Death came first, on January 26, 1963, in Naples.

Notes:
I strongly recommend "The Case against Lucky Luciano" by Ellen Poulson, for an in-depth examination of his prostitution conviction.

The events surrounding Luciano's wartime experience, his pardon, and deportation are best examined in, "The Luciano Project" by Rodney Campbell.

I dismiss the theory that Luciano was involved in the drug trade in Italy let alone being the mastermind behind international trafficking.

I utterly reject the legitimacy of "The Last Testament of Lucky Luciano" by Martin A. Gosch and Richard Hammer. So too does the FBI.

STEFANO MAGADDINO

Like so many early members of La Cosa Nostra, Magaddino came from a background of conflict in his hometown of Castellammare del Golfo, in Sicily. He was part of a clan that included relatives from the Bonanno, Bonventre, and Magaddino families. They were involved in an on and off, bloody dispute with the Buccellatos, that eventually spilled over into America.

In February of 1909, Magaddino arrived in New York and began his journey to the top of La Cosa Nostra. Like so many other Italian immigrants, Magaddino already had family and friends in the Big Apple so assimilation mustn't have been too difficult. Unfortunately, the conflict from his hometown was also playing out in New York. This likely caused him great concern for his personal family.

This MAY explain his travel to Chicago, whose Mafia Family was then controlled by the powerful Anthony D'Andrea. Many years later, in the early 1960s, an illegal FBI bug, hidden in Magaddino's funeral home office, recorded Magaddino detailing the fact that he was "made" (inducted) into the Mafia by D'Andrea.

Magaddino was seeking protection from the Buccellatos. By being formally recognized as a made member of the Mafia, and especially under the wing of the much-feared D'Andrea, Magaddino would have achieved that goal.

Back in Brooklyn, Magaddino was surrounded by many men from his hometown. Among them were; Gaspar Milazzo, the future Boss of Detroit, and Salvatore Sabella, later Boss of Philadelphia. These men and others began forming the foundation of a Family that later became known as the Bonannos.

In the fall of 1921, Magaddino got jammed up in a well-publicized murder case. The body of Camillo Caizzo was found in New Jersey, and it wasn't long before Bartolo Fontana was detained. He quickly folded like a house of cards.

Fontana admitted to the murder and claimed it was ordered by a group called "The Good Killers." Not long afterward, Magaddino and others were arrested in New York. They were held for extradition to New Jersey to face questioning on the killing.

Greatly exaggerated, fear creating stories began appearing in the press making it seem as if a group of killers was roaming the United States murdering at will. It was nonsense.

In time, the authorities dropped Magaddino from the case. After that Magaddino made his way to Buffalo where he had lots of connections. Many of them were with the top levels of that Family.

Buffalo Boss Giuseppe DiCarlo had died of natural causes on July 9, 1922. When Magaddino put down roots that fall the Family was in turmoil over who would become the next Boss. A reasonable guess would be that the feuding factions settled on Magaddino as a compromise candidate. On a secret FBI recording in the mid-1960s, Magaddino claimed he never wanted the top job and was forced into it.

According to Bonanno, Stefano Magaddino continued to have considerable influence over his former Family in Brooklyn. Bonanno wrote, "The Brooklyn Family was left in the hands of Cola Shiro, a bland, compliant man who depended on my cousin Stefano for his position."

During the Castellammarese War, Magaddino refused Masseria's demand that he appear before him in New York. Magaddino then basically hunkered down in Buffalo and kept out of the action. He did approve the ascension of Maranzano to the Bonanno Family throne. According to Valachi, Magaddino sent $5,000 to Maranzano each week. This contribution was to help cover the cost of paying those who were actively involved in combat.

By the time the Commission was formed, in 1931, Magaddino was a significant power. He had interests in bootlegging, gambling, extortion, narcotics trafficking, and a whole host of other illegal activities. Magaddino maintained close connections to leaders in Philadelphia, New York, Detroit, and Pittston. He also knew countless other influential La Cosa Nostra members. Few significant decisions of national importance could be made without his input.

It was not all champagne and roses for the next thirty years. A bomb, mistakenly thrown into the house next to him, killed his sister. In 1954, Magaddino felt compelled to demote his Underboss for some severe infraction.

Two years later, on January 11, 1956, the humiliated man, Angelo Acquisto, killed himself. Then, the newly installed Underboss, Sam Pieri, got jammed up on narcotics charges and went away to serve a long sentence.

But, the worst news for Magaddino, in the 1950s, was the fiasco on November 14, 1957, near Apalachin, New York. State Troopers had accidentally come upon a National Meeting of La Cosa Nostra. Magaddino lucked out in that he was not caught. The presence of his clothing clearly suggested he was on his way. Magaddino had dodged a bullet.

In hindsight, it is likely that Magaddino would just have soon skipped the 1960s. Although he didn't know it, the FBI had succeeded in bugging his office on November 8, 1962. Then a very major dispute arose between Joe Bonanno and other Bosses with Magaddino deeply involved. This event and the Apalachin fiasco will be discussed in more detail later in the book.

Things began to fall apart in 1968. The FBI conducted a series of gambling raids on the major players in Magaddino's Family. They found a stash of nearly $500,000 in the home of his son Peter, much to the astonishment of Magaddino's Capos and Soldiers. Their Boss had been crying poor for more than a year, and now they learned the Magaddinos were sitting on a pile of cash.

The internal discontent led to a significant split in the Family. One faction formed around former Underboss Sam Pieri. They declared themselves the new rulers of the Buffalo Family. Meanwhile, Magaddino's crew in Rochester split off and formed their own, new Family. Neither action was blessed by the Commission, till the death of Magaddino on July 19, 1974.

Magaddino's long run had ended in turmoil and humiliation.

CHAPTER FIVE

Forming The Commission: Part Two

ORIGINAL COMMISSION MEMBER PROFILES cont'd

JOSEPH BONANNO

We are fortunate that the egos of Joe Bonanno and his son Bill caused them to produce books, magazine articles and make TV appearances as they tried to generate money and defend their lives in La Cosa Nostra. With the addition of primary source materials, a reasonably accurate profile of Bonanno, an original Commission member, can be constructed.

Bonanno was born in Castellammare del Golfo on January 18, 1905. He was born into the Mafia life as his grandfather, uncles, father, and others were, at various times, head of that city's Family.

In 1908, Bonanno and his immediate family moved to New York, only to return to Sicily four years later. Violence had begun to escalate in Castellammare del Golfo once again. Bonanno's father was needed back home.

For the next twelve years, Bonanno's life was one of Mafia conflict, failures in education, and confusion about his future. Finally, in 1924, Bonanno and Peter Magaddino decided to immigrate to America. After a long journey, which included the last stop in Cuba, Bonanno illegally entered the US and made his way to New York City.

Bonanno's blood connection to the powerful Stefano Magaddino of Buffalo made his integration into the Castellammarese community a reasonably easy one. Before long, Bonanno was producing illegal whiskey from his own still and wearing better clothes. Unfortunately, an accident with the still killed his partner, Giovanni Romano. Consequently, Bonanno moved into the legal field. His uncle, Vito Bonventre, put him to work driving a bakery truck.

That sojourn was short-lived, for the famous Salvatore Maranzano had arrived in New York, in 1925. He had immediately been taken into the Bonanno Family, then headed by Cola Shiro. Before long, Bonanno was acting as Maranzano's right-hand man and trouble-shooter.

According to Bonanno, his primary focus was on ensuring that the still operations that Maranzano controlled ran smoothly. He claimed that there were both mundane jobs to be done, along with the periodic use of threats and sometimes extreme violence. For Bonanno, this was a great life.

We've already detailed the significant events of the rise and fall of Maranzano so we'll skip ahead to a brief rundown of the most significant occurrences in Bonanno's long reign.

In 1931, Bonanno became both the head of his own Family and an original member of the Commission. With this power, things went very smoothly, up until the 1950s. As we'll detail later, a series of power struggles in New York, led to both intrigue, conspiracies, and violence. Heads would roll. Eventually, Bonanno fell entirely out of favor and was officially expelled from his Boss position, his seat on the Commission, and his membership in La Cosa Nostra.

At first, Bonanno tried to regain his positions, but these attempts failed. By 1968, he was sulking in his Tucson, Arizona home. At this point, he began phoning old friends from around the nation and up in Montreal. This made the FBI curious as to just what his status was. In time, they put a full court press on him, which led to a series of problems.

BOMBS AWAY

Although it is hard to believe, in the late 1960s, Bonanno, and other Mafia figures in the Tucson area, were subjected to a series of bombings allegedly orchestrated by an FBI agent named David Hale. Thankfully, no one was killed, and the truth finally came out. Some participants were convicted, but Hale skated although his career in the FBI was over. To date, no evidence has surfaced that Hale's superiors ordered this harassment campaign. Below is a brief summary of the significant events during this period.

July 21/68
The Arizona home of Detroit mobster Peter Licavoli was bombed by a small group.

July 22/68
A bomb was used against the fence of Bonanno's Tucson home, and another was tossed into the backyard. Bill Bonanno wounded one of the bombers with a shotgun.

August 16/68
The Arizona home of Bonanno Associate Peter Notaro, was bombed.

September 68
The Wig Beauty Salon in Tucson was bombed. The ex-wife of Bonanno Soldier Charles Battaglia worked there.

July 21/69
Tucson police arrested Paul M Stevens, in connection with the bombing of Joe Bonanno's home.

July 23/69
Tucson police arrested William J Dunbar, for being involved with the bombing of Bonanno's home

August 12/69
David Hale resigned from the FBI. The same day, Dunbar and Stevens were in court, in Tucson, and Hale's name came up.

UNWANTED PUBLICITY

In 1971, "Honor Thy Father," by Gay Talese, was published. It was basically the life story of Bill Bonanno as he moved through the Mafia troubles of the 1960s, combined with a history of the Mafia, as it was known at that time. Joe Bonanno was not pleased. He said he didn't speak to Bill for more than a year. When the made for TV movie came out, Joe Bonanno's anger must have only grown.

THE PERSECUTION ERA

During this period, Bonanno was subjected to a series of aggressive manoeuvers, which in hindsight, look very petty. Unfortunately, he had become a target due to his national notoriety. Ambitious prosecutors, federal agents and local police authorities wanted his scalp as a trophy. They leaked their version of the truth to a gullible media who splashed the stories over the airways, in the newspapers and magazines. It was ridiculous, for Bonanno had less than zero power. Unfortunately, he still possessed a gigantic ego and a burning desire to prove to the public that his life was a noble one.

Below are some of the significant events of this period of time.

June 2/76
A bomb in his car killed Arizona Republic reporter Don Bolles. The media was outraged and soon began a series of stories focusing on crime in Arizona. These created a poisonous atmosphere and directed hate towards the Mafia figures like Bonanno. It was unfair and especially when it turned out that the hit had nothing to do with the Mafia.

June 1978
A Penthouse article, naming Bonanno as the real Godfather, was published. This tale was beyond ridiculous. It claimed that Bonanno still controlled his family in New York and was the head guy in a massive drug trafficking conspiracy with connections all over the nation. The trouble was that there was no evidence to support this version of events. It was entirely unfair to Bonanno and the gullible public.

March 17/79
Arizona law enforcement agents raided Bonanno's Tucson home. They confiscate the draft copy of his autobiography.

September 2/80
Joe Bonanno and nephew Jack DeFilippi were convicted of obstruction of justice in a bankruptcy case involving his son.

February 81
Bonanno won $6000 in a suit against two former Tucson cops, who illegally tapped his phone.

December 5/83
Bonanno began serving his obstruction of justice sentence.

July 27/84
Bonanno was released from his prison sentence. It had been reduced to one year from five due to his health.

TO BE CONTINUED

Bonanno's profile will be continued in a later chapter where his direct connection to the Commission case will be discussed.

VINCENT MANGANO

There isn't a lot of information on the early years of Mangano's life in the United States, after arriving from Sicily. We do know that he was about 42 when he went through the long lines at Ellis Island and a reasonable assumption would be that he was at least familiar with the ways of the Mafia.

From his life in the nineteen thirties and forties, we can suggest that, upon his arrival, he quickly linked up with members of the D'Aquila Family (Gambino) who controlled the docks in Brooklyn. His power and status had to have made a great leap for him to become a Boss and a Commission member in 1931.

RISING TO THE TOP

As discussed previously, Boss of Bosses Salvatore D'Aquila was an avowed enemy of Joe Masseria. D'Aquila was betrayed by his Underboss, Al Mineo, in 1928. Mineo assumed the throne of the Gambino Family, with Masseria's blessing. Mangano must have been pretty nimble on his feet to have survived this coup. His power continued to grow.

As the Castellammarese War began to tilt in Maranzano's favor, some of the Mineo Family (Gambino) started jumping ship. Boss Al Mineo and Underboss Steve Ferrigno were gunned down on November 5, 1930. Capo Frank Scalise broke ranks and joined the Maranzano army, quickly followed by Mangano.

After Masseria was killed, in April of 1931, Frank Scalise took over the Gambino Family. Maranzano supported his move. One of Scalise's first orders, from Maranzano, was that he kill Mangano who was not trusted by Maranzano. Scalise stalled, according to Gentile, who wrote, "Because Cicco Scalise did not carry through with the promised action, which was the elimination of Mangano…" Mangano was saved by Scalise's inaction, but would not entirely benefit from his benevolence.

In September of 1931, Maranzano was whacked out and his favorite, Scalise, became vulnerable. According to Bonanno, the Gambino Family made a smart move and elected the respected Mangano as their new Boss. On top of that, Bonanno wrote, "We selected Vincent Mangano to chair our (Commission) meetings." It had been a rocket ride to the top of the Mafia heap for Mangano.

TROUBLE IN PITTSBURGH

Mangano's throne just about came crashing down, on July 29, 1932. Three Volpe brothers were whacked out in an ambush in Pittsburgh. It had been organized by Pittsburgh Boss John Bazzano. Their close friend, the ferocious Vito Genovese, was confident Mangano, Albert Anastasia, and Joe Biondo were behind the slaughter. Genovese was on the warpath.

Fortunately, the suspects learned of the plans of Genovese and convinced him to delay. Meanwhile, they tried to get to the bottom of the incident. Bazzano was told to come to New York immediately.

Once the group gathered, Bazzano was anything but remorseful. He angrily said that they should kill all the Neapolitans (Genovese was Neopolitan). Seeing that there was no reasoning with the volatile Bazzano, Genovese et al. killed him. His body was stuffed in a sack and dumped in the street. Bazzano's corpse was found on August 7, 1932. Genovese was appeased, but he really didn't buy the innocence story of Mangano, Anastasia, and Biondo.

TROUBLE IN PITTSBURGH 2

With the death of Pittsburgh Boss Bazzano, Vincent Capizzi was elected as the replacement. He selected Frank Amato as his Underboss, with Nicola Gentile acting as Consigliere. Things went south quickly.

Capizzi ordered the death of a Capo, which Gentile opposed. Capizzi and Amato then traveled to New York to complain about the behavior of Gentile. Genovese was already suspicious that Gentile had played a role in the murders of the Volpe brothers. He then approved the killing of Gentile.

Fortunately for Gentile, his friends in the Gambino Family got wind of the plot and urged him to travel to New York. Gentile met with Vince Mangano, Albert Anastasia, and Joe Biondo, the entire administration of the Gambino Family. Vito Genovese also joined the discussion, along with Capizzi and Amato.

Anastasia quickly solved the problem by saying that Gentile was now a member of the Gambino Family and ordered Capizzi to prepare the transfer papers. This first-hand account from Gentile gives us an insider view of a real Mafia sit-down.

MAFIA INTRIGUE

Lucky Luciano had been convicted of compulsory prostitution and given a lengthy sentence, on June 18, 1936. The manoeuvering for his position began immediately. Mangano was in the middle of it.

Gentile related that Vito Genovese wanted to kill a rival for Luciano's throne. The intended victim was named Dominick "Terry Burns" Didato." Probably for secrecy and support, Genovese brought Mangano in on the plot, even though they were members of different Families.

Perhaps, this was a Commission approved hit, which might explain the two Family attack. In any case, Terry Burns was taken out efficiently. Unfortunately for Genovese, the way was not clear to the throne. He had a murder investigation on his heels. Genovese high footed it to Italy in 1937.

DODGING A BULLET

Many followers of Mafia history are well aware of Abe Reles, "The Canary Who Could Sing but Couldn't Fly." For those who don't know this name, a brief summary is in order.

Reles was one of many violent Jewish gangsters, who battered their way around Brooklyn, killing anyone who got in their way. During his journey, Reles was involved in some Mafia ordered murders. Finally, someone started to talk, with the result that Reles made a sprint to the good guys. He too began to speak. His revelations were a media sensation and spawned countless news stories, books, and movies. This is not the time to examine those events, other than to describe one that is linked to Mangano.

Bookie Irving "Puggy" Feinstein was found dead on September 4, 1939. A year later, Reles was on the stand, giving his version of this hit. He claimed the order came from Albert Anastasia, whom Reles referred to as "The Boss." Reles went on to explain, that Anastasia was passing on the kill order on behalf of Vincent Mangano. Feinstein had to go "because he crossed Vince," said Reles from his perch in the courtroom.

Luckily for Mangano and Anastasia, Reles later took his famous flight out of a sixth-floor window of the Half Moon Hotel on Coney Island, while under police protection. Mangano and many others must have breathed sighs of relief.

ON THE WATERFRONT

On April 21, 1940, The Brooklyn Daily Eagle newspaper published an in-depth story on their investigations about matters on the waterfront. It was not a pretty story.

The article claimed that Mangano, "had charge of all the waterfront rackets, in the area between Brooklyn Bridge and 52 Street in Bay Ridge. It went on to describe Mangano as "shrewd and intelligent" and that "he ruled with an iron hand." Their investigation revealed that Mangano, "has issued most of his orders... through subordinates. He has had little contact with the minor mobsters and is now a wealthy man."

ON THE WATERFRONT 2

Ten years later, the newspaper was reporting the same story. On December 12, 1950, the Brooklyn Eagle claimed that Mangano was still ruling all the Brooklyn docks. The article listed the six Locals, of the International Longshoremen's Association, under the thumb of Mangano and his flunkies.

Another interesting piece of information in the story was that Mangano was involved in the "City Democratic Club," which has been in existence since 1932. No doubt, this "Club" was closely linked to the powerful Tammany Hall organization that controlled much of the New York political process for decades.

HERE COMES TROUBLE

Albert Anastasia was Mangano's Underboss, but also his rival. Both men were powers on the docks and were thus vying for the same piece of the pie.

Bonanno wrote that Mangano, "had to be especially wary of Anastasia." He also added that "Albert's ambition did not sit well with Mangano." Clearly, this situation could not continue. It will be examined in a later chapter.

CHAPTER SIX

Forming The Commission: Part Three

ORIGINAL COMMISSION MEMBER PROFILES cont'd

GIUSEPPE "JOE" PROFACI

Of all the original Commission members, Profaci's early years in New York are the most mysterious. Documents show that he arrived in New York on September 4, 1921, when he was 24 years old. He next appeared in Chicago, making a vain attempt to run a grocery store. At that point, Profaci returned to New York to make a meteoric rise to the heights of La Cosa Nostra.

Like so many other LCN members in the early days, Profaci was no stranger to the courtroom in Italy. In later testimony, he admitted to being charged with a crime but released in 1916. Four years later, he spent a year in prison on minor charges. Thus, we have no evidence of a background of violence, although that is always possible. We do not have a lot of documentation of his life in his hometown of Villabate, Sicily.

On September 27, 1927, Profaci was naturalized in New York. Two years later, he married Nina Magliocco, whose brother Giuseppe would become

Profaci's life-time Underboss. Other than that, how he became the leader of a powerful Mafia Family continues to be a frustrating mystery.

THE FAMOUS MAFIA ENCLAVE IN CLEVELAND

On December 5, 1928, Profaci, Underboss Joseph Magliocco and 21 others were arrested by Cleveland police at the Statler Hotel. The good guys had received a tip that the Capone gang was meeting in Cleveland. 50 officers raided the hotel and took Profaci et al. into custody, as being "suspicious persons."

Probably in a panic, the newly minted Boss of Cleveland, Joe Porello, put together the finances to bail each of the men out on $10,000 bonds. Before that happened, the cops took a group photograph, along with mugshots. 13 pistols were confiscated and proudly displayed for the media.

Refusing to plead guilty as 15 others had, both Profaci and Magliocco went to trial on December 15, 1928. They were found not guilty and released the same day.

This event has taken its place at the high levels of La Cosa Nostra history and is frequently referred to in books, magazines, and in mob documentaries. The trouble is that the exact reason for this mob gathering remained elusive. The following paragraphs will end that uncertainty.

When you look at where the men were from, the reason for the location becomes evident. Most of the detained were from Chicago, and the other key figures like Profaci and Vincent Mangano were out of New York. Back in the days of doing most of your traveling by road or rail, Cleveland was a "midway" stop between the two cities.

Highly respected mob historian David Critchley probably comes closest as to the reason for the gathering. Powerful mobster Frankie Yale had been whacked out on July 1, 1928. He was a Capo in the Masseria (Genovese) Family and intimately connected to Capone, the architect of his murder. His sphere of influence was mainly in Brooklyn, where Profaci's Family was located.

For Critchley, the purposes of the meeting were to introduce Profaci as the Boss of a new Family and to get Chicago's recognition of this fact. Furthermore, since Profaci would now most likely begin to assimilate Yale's Brooklyn rackets, Chicago's acceptance of this would be an extremely positive move.

We can also conclude that if these were the primary reasons for the conference, Joe Masseria, still Capone's Boss, must have given his blessing. He recognized Profaci as a new Boss. He also agreed to Profaci taking over the Yale rackets. Masseria was always looking for allies.

PROFACI'S ROLE IN THE CASTELLAMMARESE WAR

Unfortunately, we are unable to give a definitive description of what Profaci and his Family did in the Castellammarese War that ended the reign of Boss of Bosses Joe Masseria. We have two conflicting versions.

According to Valachi, Profaci was actually part of a stake-out team looking to kill Masseria. Valachi wrote, "One of the guys who stays on and off in my apartment is Joe Profaci, and he explains a lot of the history of what has been going on." Later, Valachi explained that "Joe Profaci had given me Mr. Maranzano's pedigree. Finally, Valachi claimed that Profaci was present when Maranzano inducted Valachi and a group of other new recruits into La Cosa Nostra.

Bonanno dismissed Valachi's version. He wrote, "Often he (Valachi) described historical events in which he never participated, but nonetheless inserted himself to make himself seem important to his gullible audience."

Bonanno claimed that "His (Profaci) Family would never take part in the war directly. Maranzano urged Profaci to remain officially neutral and to act as an intermediary with other groups."

Admittedly there is not a lot of evidence about Profaci's role in the war, but Valachi's version rings true. Especially when you consider that Bonanno vehemently denied that he was chosen as Valachi's "Godfather" at his induction. He was lying. It was abhorrent for Bonanno to be linked to Valachi in any way and thus he denigrated everything the famous turncoat ever said. The conclusion has to be that the Profaci Family was active in the Castellammarese War.

PROFACI'S ROLE IN THE DEATH OF MARANZANO

Once again, there is little-known evidence about Profaci's role in the murder of Maranzano. Valachi tells us that Dominick "The Gap" Petrilli took him out partying the day Maranzano was killed. For Valachi, this indicated that Petrilli, a close Associate of Thomas Gagliano, the Boss of the Lucchese Family, was aware of the plot and was trying to save Valachi from harm. It is safe to assume that if low-level Soldier Petrilli knew, then Profaci, a Boss who continued to reign after the hit, was also in the loop.

PROFACI'S PERSONAL LIFE

There was always something going on in Profaci's own life that took up a lot of his time and attention. Below are some of the highlights.

Olive Oil
Profaci owned and operated companies that distributed olive oil. In 1949, he pleaded guilty to altering the product.

Taxes
In 1953, the US Attorney moved to liquidate some Profaci companies/properties, to pay off more than $2 million, allegedly owed by Profaci in company taxes and penalties. Profaci was also indicted for owing $88,000 in personal taxes.

A marshal's sale of Profaci holdings was held in 1960. A number of the properties were bought by Profaci relatives, and companies linked to him for fire-sale prices.

Deportation
After the Kefauver Hearings of the early 1950s, the government started using expulsion as a means to handle their Mafia problem. In 1954, Profaci became a target. After a denaturalization trial in 1958, Profaci was ordered deported. An Appeal Court vacated this order, in January 1960.

Marriages
In the mid-1950s, Profaci's two daughters married sons of the leaders of the Detroit Mafia. Carmella wed Anthony Zerilli, while her sister, Antoinette, joined hands with Giacomo "Jack" Tocco. Both of these men would later be Bosses.

After the accidental death of Profaci's brother Salvatore, Profaci took his children under his protection. Niece Rosalie would eventually marry Salvatore "Bill" Bonanno, son of Joe Bonanno.

Health
Profaci's health had always been reasonably good, although he smashed up his leg just before the fateful 1928 Cleveland meeting. Trouble really began in October of 1958. Profaci was admitted to the hospital complaining of headaches. He returned a month later with the same problem. In hindsight, we know these were the first signs of his brain tumor. His gallbladder was removed in 1962, followed shortly after that by his death on June 6, 1962.

Personality
In her book, "Mafia Marriage", Rosalie Bonanno (nee Profaci) gave this profile of her uncle Joe. She wrote, "He was a flamboyant man who smoked big cigars, drove big black Cadillacs, and did things like buy tickets to a Broadway play for us cousins." She went on to explain that he didn't buy two or three tickets but a whole row.

PROFACI'S MAFIA LIFE AFTER 1931

Profaci became one of the original members of the Commission in 1931. By the 1950s, the Mafia was in the limelight, and things were happening fast and furiously, with Profaci right in the center of the storm. These events will be described in later chapters.

TOMMASO "TOMMY" GAGLIANO

Like most of the original members of the Commission, Gagliano was involved in some semi-legitimate endeavors besides being Boss of the Lucchese Family.

Gagliano was from the city made famous by the Godfather movies, Corleone Sicily. Some sources indicate that he may have been involved in Mafia activities there before he immigrated to the United States.

GAGLIANO'S BUSINESS LIFE

From primary source material, we know Gagliano was heavily involved in the construction industry in the Bronx and more specifically, in what today would be called the drywall business. Valachi said, "He (Gagliano) was in construction work." That foothold led to the formation of an association of area companies involved in the same business. This entity was called, "The Plaster's Information Bureau." In simple terms, it was a vehicle for extortion. It was highly successful, according to the government.

In February of 1932, Gagliano and others were indicted for tax evasion on $1,270,000 that they extorted and didn't report. That is the equivalent of over $20,000,000 in today's dollars. This was the big time. Later that year, Gagliano was sentenced to 15 months in the slammer. It is not clear how much time he served if any.

GAGLIANO'S MAFIA POLITICS

Gagliano associated with the Tommy Reina (Lucchese) Family whose main base was in the Bronx. At some point, Reina promoted Gagliano to Underboss.

A Masseria inspired coup resulted in Reina's death, on February 26, 1930. Joe Pinzollo, a Masseria puppet, was installed in his place at which point Gagliano and others then broke away from the Family. These "rebels" whacked out Joe Pinzollo on September 3, 1930. Gagliano et al. then moved into an alliance with Maranzano. Not long afterwards, Gagliano was elected Boss of the Reina (Lucchese) Family.

Gagliano approved the recruiting of Valachi and a number of his friends to help fight against Masseria. He was also present when Valachi and others were inducted into La Cosa Nostra. This was after the successful killings of Masseria allies, Al Mineo and Steve Ferrigno (Gambino Family). Valachi also claimed that Gagliano attended his wedding.

FINALLY

Unfortunately, Gagliano exits our stage at this point except for a few appearances of little consequence to our story. Clearly, this leaves a considerable gap in our understanding of his life, but it will be up to others to continue searching.

CHAPTER SEVEN

Forming The Commission: Part Four

ORIGINAL COMMISSION MEMBER PROFILES cont'd

AL CAPONE

Capone is still the most famous gangster in American history, nearly eighty-six years after he went off to prison and out of the headlines. It has been seventy-one years since his death on January 25, 1947, but he is still present in films, TV shows, books, and other media. It's almost like he never went away.

This original Commission member was born in New York City on January 17, 1899, becoming a member of the large and expanding Capone family. For Alphonse, school was not for him, and he was roaming the streets at 14.

MAKING CONNECTIONS

During the next few years, he bounced around doing factory work, but these were short-lived ventures. The critical moves occurred when he came into the orbit of a young Johnny Torrio, who was quietly running some rackets in Brooklyn. Then Capone met Frankie Yale, a powerful gangster whose headquarters was at the Harvard Inn in Coney Island. These two men would play critical roles in the rise of Capone.

The young Capone worked as a waiter/bouncer for Yale. During this period Capone received the three scars on the left side of his face that gave him the famous name "Scarface." Capone insulted a young lady, and her brother took exception to it. A fight broke out, and Capone was slashed three times with a small knife. The perpetrator fled but was smart enough to seek support.

That backing came in the form of Lucky Luciano, already a force to be reckoned with. Fortunately for Capone, his connection to both Torrio and Yale saved him.

In an attempt to lead a calmer life, Capone got married on Dec 30, 1918, and soon afterward moved to Baltimore, where he worked as a bookkeeper for a construction company. This tranquility would only last till January of 1921, when he accepted an invitation from his old mentor, Johnny Torrio, to join him in Chicago. Fame, fortune, and danger were right around the corner.

According to Joe Bonanno, Capone had gone to Chicago, "...with the consent of Frankie Yale... a group leader in Masseria's Family, and it can be assumed that Capone's relocation to Chicago had the blessing of 'Joe the Boss.'"

CHICAGO: EARLY YEARS

When Capone arrived in Chicago, his mentor, Johnny Torrio was running the vice empire of the late Jim "Big Jim" Colosimo. The latter had been gunned down, on May 11, 1920, in his famous "Colosimo Café." This hit paved the way for Torrio to move to the top. It is reasonable to assume that the advent of Prohibition and all its possibilities, played a role in Torrio's decision to carry out a coup. Although there were/are suspects as to who the shooter was, it can definitely be said it wasn't Capone. He was still in Baltimore working with figures when the hit went down.

Before long, Capone was running the Four Deuces speakeasy. It doubled as the headquarters of the Torrio empire and a place where you could buy both a drink and the services of a call girl. Capone was at the center of a conglomerate of many brothels, countless speakeasies, and other rackets. From this joint, decisions were made as to which politicians and cops were to be paid off. Capone was Torrio's right-hand man.

THE RIVALS

Not surprisingly, in the wild days of Prohibition, many gangs sprang up eager to cash in on the gold rush. The competition was fierce leading to great bursts of violence and bodies in the streets. The Capone gang was always under siege whether due to attacks on their territory or when they tried to expand their operations. Many lived hard and died young. Below are brief descriptions of Capone's main rivals and the significant actions that occurred.

Note:
In 1920 Torrio formed an agreement with the significant bootleggers in Chicago. Territories were assigned, and pledges made to respect these lines.

THE O'BANION/WIESS/MORAN GANG

O'Banion was an interesting gangster in that he had an artistic side which he displayed in his floral arrangement created in his own flower shop. As mild-mannered as he appeared, O'Banion was tough enough to have carved out a highly successful bootlegging and hijacking operation in Chicago's North End.

O'Banion had a series of agreements with Torrio/Capone, such as holding a one-third interest with them in the Sieben Brewery. The two groups generally respected each other's territory, but tensions were rising in 1924.

In hindsight, O'Banion made some errors. Torrio had given him permission to take over a small area in Cicero, a neighboring town near Chicago that the Torrio/Capone gang controlled lock stock and barrel. Something went south with this arrangements and Torrio filed it away for future reference.

Then another group began selling a rotgut product in O'Banion's north side territory. He appealed to Torrio for support, but the Boss rebuffed him. O'Banion was seething inside.

O'Banion suddenly announced that he was retiring from the rackets. He was willing to sell his share in the Sieben Brewery to his partners Torrio and Capone. The duo jump at the chance to be rid of the troublesome O'Banion and agreed to the deal.

On May 19, 1924, Torrio and O'Banion were at the Brewery while the last shipment under the trios' supervision arrived. Suddenly the good guys swept in and arrested everyone. This was big trouble for Torrio for he already had a record. Later he pled guilty and was given a nine-month sentence and a fine. Both he and Capone were very suspicious of the circumstances of this raid and started digging for the truth. This would not be good for O'Banion.

O'Banion met his maker on November 10, 1924. Three gunmen entered the store and were greeted by the gangster/florist. O'Banion was next seen sprawled on the floor as the result of six bullets being fired into him. His death was headline news, and the funeral was spectacular. However, the bottom line was that O'Banion was dead.

Most accounts lay the blame for the killing on an alliance of the Capone gang and that of the Genna brothers. That conclusion is logical, but there was no substantial evidence to support it. Everyone skated legal problems. That didn't satisfy O'Banion's partners. They vowed revenge. That would turn out to be another miscalculation.

O'Banion loyalists, led by Hymie Weis, Vincent "Schemer" Drucci, and Bug Moran, began a violent war against the Torrio/Capone gang. The highlights are listed below. There were many other actions taking place during this same period that are not covered.

January 12/25
Capone's vehicle was shot up in Cicero. Capone had just left the car. Shooters were thought to have been Weiss, Drucci, and Moran.

January 24/25
Torrio was shot as he and his wife arrived at their apartment in a Weiss/Moran attack. He survived but shortly after Torrio "retired" and turned the organization over to the eager Capone.

August10/26
Weiss and Drucci were ambushed by Capone gunmen in front of the Standard Oil Building, 910 South Michigan Ave. They survived.

August 15/26
Weiss and Drucci were attacked by Capone gunmen as they drove by the Standard Oil Building. Again they survived.

September 10/26
The Capone headquarters, at the Hawthorne Inn in Cicero, was shot up in a brazen, extremely violent attack. Capone was not hit.

October 11/26
Weiss was finally killed in a machine gun ambush.

October 1926
Drucci and Moran tentatively made peace with Capone.

April 4/27
Drucci was arrested for carrying a concealed gun. He got into
a verbal fight with one of the officers. The cop killed Drucci with
a pistol shot.

THE SAINT VALENTINES DAY MASSACRE

This event is the most famous massacre in the history of the American
mob. Technically it was not a La Cosa Nostra matter for Capone had not yet
entered into that fabled organization. But it was still a massacre.

The O'Banion/Weiss/Drucci gang was now led by the less than competent
George "Bugs" Moran. They continued to be an irritant and danger to the
Capone organization. One of their most provocative acts was the attempted
murder of the famous Jack "Machine Gun" McGurn, a long- time Capone
hitman. The Capones decided to end the problem once and for all. Plans
were made, and Capone gave his approval from his vacation perch in Miami.

The fatal day would be February 14, 1929. Moran and his crew were lured
to their garage headquarters with the promise of a lucrative bootlegging deal.
A fake police car pulled up disgorging two uniformed officers and two other
men in suits. The four rushed into the garage and soon had seven men lined
up against a wall. Presumably, the occupants thought this was a harmless
raid. They were wrong.

The four "cops" unloaded the magazines of two machine guns, a shotgun,
and some rounds from a .45 automatic pistol into the six unsuspecting Moran
gang members and one groupie. It was ugly, as the bodies were really torn up
with blood and guts everywhere.

Witnesses saw two men, dressed in suits, with their hands up, being led
out of the garage by the two uniformed cops. It looked like an arrest. The men
sped off, and no one was ever charged for this terrible massacre.

Seven men were dead, but Moran had been late and therefore was still
breathing. However, he would no longer be a threat to Capone and quickly
faded into the life of a common criminal. "Capone" by Lawrence Bergreen
gives an excellent account of this event and the entire life of Capone.

CAPONE JOINS LA COSA NOSTRA

The Colosimo/Torrio/Capone organization was not initially a formal La Cosa Nostra Family. To understand how Capone became a member of La Cosa Nostra and the Commission a study of Frankie Yale is necessary.

FRANKIE YALE

As discussed above, Capone was intimately connected to Brooklyn's powerful Frankie Yale, a Capo in the Masseria (Genovese) Family. Bonanno wrote that Yale must have given permission for Capone to move to Chicago. He added that Masseria had to have signed off as well. At first, the connection was good for both men but eventually it went south.

Yale had access to high-grade whiskey and had agreed to sell to Capone. Unfortunately, Capone's trucks, leaving Brooklyn, were being hijacked on a regular basis. In 1928, Capone began to suspect that Yale was double-crossing him by arranging for the hijacking of the Capone convoys.

On July 1, 1928, it all came to a head when Yale was gunned down while driving in Brooklyn. The link to Chicago came rapidly. Both the guns used and the hit vehicle were connected to Capone people. There was not enough evidence to bring anyone to court, but those in the know fully understood it was a Capone job.

More important than who the actual killers were was the question of who had approved the hit and what did it mean. It is safe to conclude that Yale's Boss, Joe Masseria, signed off on the murder. The question then became, "Why would he do that?"

As later events would indicate, it is certain that Masseria wanted to gain a considerable foothold in the gold mine of Chicago. It was clear that Capone was rapidly achieving dominance of the criminal world in that city.

When Masseria heard Capone's complaints against Yale, his decision was not a hard one. He agreed to the killing of the easily replaceable Yale, and in return, this put Capone in his debt. Yale was as good as gone.

CAPONE VERSUS THE SICILIANS

Chicago had a formal La Cosa Nostra Family that had participated in the selections of Bosses of Bosses and was most likely present at other Mafia gatherings. The Capone organization was not a formal Mafia Family at first. What follows is a brief summary of the Boss of the Chicago Family.

Anthony D'Andrea had been Boss of the Chicago Family from around 1911 till his murder on May 12, 1921. Next up was the very popular Mike Merlino. He used his considerable influence to try to keep rival bootlegging gangs from going to war with each other. Unfortunately, Merlo died of natural causes on November 8, 1924, and things started to get nasty.

According to Gentile, Anthony Lombardo was elected as the new Boss with Joe Aiello being picked as his Underboss. During this period there initially were friendly relations with the Capone organization. That changed when Lombardo suggested to Capone that he should stop sending tribute money to Masseria in New York. Masseria got wind of this unwelcome advice which put Lombardo in big trouble. He was gunned down in the street on September 7, 1928, in a very public display of Capone's power.

Some historians have attributed the Lombardo killing to others, but Gentile places the blame squarely on Capone's shoulders. Strong supporting evidence comes from the fact that around this time, Boss of Bosses Joe Masseria formally inducted Capone into La Cosa Nostra. Masseria also appointed him as one of his Capos even though Capone was located in Chicago.

Underboss Joe Aiello was the next person on the hot seat. He complained to Masseria about Capone's activities but was rebuffed. The two departed the meeting as enemies.

Aiello and his minions made numerous attempts to kill Capone but all failed. The Capone men were also out gunning for Aiello and after many misses finally killed him on October 23, 1930. The Chicago LCN Family was basically now defunct.

At this point, it was evident to Capone that the war being run by his Boss, Joe Masseria, was going downhill fast. He began plotting with Lucky Luciano and other Family Capos. On April 15, 1931, Masseria had eaten his last meal.

Capone was formally recognized as Boss of Chicago's only La Cosa Nostra Family. This was done at a General Assembly presided over by Maranzano in the spring of 1931. According to Bonanno, this is what Maranzano said, "Although Capone used to be of the Masseria faction, he now wanted peace and the enjoyment of a society of friends." Bonanno wrote, "In so many words, therefore, Maranzano recognized Capone as the head of the Chicago Family."

Only a few months later Capone was again plotting with Luciano and others. This time to take out the autocratic Maranzano. That goal was accomplished on September 10, 1931. Capone became a member of the newly formed Commission. It has been a meteoric rise. Unfortunately for Capone, it was all downhill from there.

Below is a summary of the crucial events in his life from mid-1930 till his death in 1948.

June 5/31
A Grand Jury indicted Capone on 22 counts of income tax invasion. He surrendered and was released on $50,000 bond.

June 12/31
Another Grand Jury indicted Capone for Prohibition violations. Elliot Ness was involved.

June 16/31
Capone pled guilty to tax violations. Sentencing was set for two weeks later.

July 30/31
The deal with the government for Capone to plead guilty to his tax charges fell apart. Capone pled not guilty.

September 10/31
Salvatore Maranzano was killed as the result of a plot that included Capone.

September 1931
Capone was selected as a member of the Commission.

October 6/31
Capone's tax trial began. The jury panel was switched to negate a bribery attempt by Capone minions.

October 17/31
Capone was found not guilty on the first tax indictment but was convicted on 5 of 23 counts in the second.

October 24/31
Capone was sentenced to a total of 11 years for his tax conviction.

He was fined $50,000 and $7,692 for court costs. Capone also owed $215,000 plus interest, on back taxes. Bail was denied, and Capone was sent to Cook County Jail.

October 26/31
Capone's appeal to the US 7th Circuit Court failed.

February 27/32
Another Capone appeal was denied.

May 2/32
The Supreme Court refused to hear an appeal of Capone's tax conviction

May 3/32
Capone left Cook County Jail for Atlanta

May 4/32
Capone arrived in Atlanta to begin a ten-year federal sentence. He also owed one year in the Cook County Jail.

August 18/34
Capone was ordered to Alcatraz from Atlanta.

August 19/34
Capone left Atlanta by a train heading for Alcatraz

August 22/34
Capone arrived at Alcatraz

February 5/38
Capone was obviously ill. This was a result of him contacting syphilis as a teenager and never getting it treated adequately. The disease was now damaging his brain.

January 6/39
Capone left Alcatraz, still owing a year, and was taken to Terminal Island. There Capone was supposed to serve the one year he owed to Chicago's Cook County Jail.

November 1939
In an agreement with the Capone family, the feds decided to transfer Capone to Lewisburg prison in Pennsylvania. Once there he would be released to go to a hospital.

November 16/39
Capone arrived in Lewisburg prison for release formalities. He was immediately taken to Baltimore's Union Memorial Hospital

for treatment. Capone lived in Baltimore till the spring and went to the hospital as an outpatient.

March 22/40
Capone arrived at his Florida home

January 25/47
Capone died but became a legend.

CHAPTER EIGHT

The Commission Rules: Part One

The purposes of the Commission were outlined in the indictment that was examined in chapter one. From 1931 till 1986, there must have been hundreds of Commission meetings where a wide variety of topics were addressed. It would be nice if we had the minutes of all those gatherings, but the Mafia doesn't operate that way.

Fortunately, from sources, we have a few instances in which Mafia members discussed Commission matters. Using these small bits, combined with historical knowledge of La Cosa Nostra, we are able to draw a reasonable conclusion as to just what was happening in these snapshots.

APPROVING THE INDUCTION OF NEW MEMBERS

The rule was implemented to prevent war in New York, which was always a tinderbox due to the presence of five competing Families. The membership of each New York Family was frozen at their 1931 levels. This was referred to as, "The books are closed."

In 1988, Cleveland's Angelo Lonardo, a former Acting Boss, told a Senate Committee, "…but there was a freeze on after that. You couldn't make any members." Back in 1963, Joe Valachi told another Senate Committee the same thing, "…the books were closed in about 1931 and were re-opened around 1954."

The Genovese and Gambino Families were then and are now the largest. Their 1931 membership has been estimated at 300 formal members each. The other three Families (Bonanno, Lucchese, and Colombo) were around the 100 mark per Family.

It was the Commission's job to ensure that those ratios continued into the future, and they have, although membership has dropped dramatically in all five Families.

This rule had to take into consideration that members died of natural causes or might be killed. As a consensus grew that the ranks were being depleted or getting too old, the Commission would, "Open the Books" which meant that a process to approve new members could begin.

Each New York Family would know how many members they were allowed to induct. Let's use ten for this explanation. Each Family would draw up a list of ten recently deceased members along with the year of their death. They'd add the names and nicknames of their ten proposed members. The names would then be circulated among the other four Families.

The purpose of this exercise was to eliminate any possibility that someone might object to a proposed member. The Commission was attempting to cut off any potential interfamily conflict at an early stage. Once the person was "made" (inducted) a whole new set of protocols clicked in making things much more complicated.

PROOF OF THE APPROVAL RULE

JOHN GOTTI JR.

These induction lists were known to the good guys for decades thanks to informers and bugs. However, the carelessness of John Gotti Junior of the Gambino Family put concrete evidence of their existence into the hands of the FBI. In a raid on a property controlled by Gotti Junior, copies of the lists from one "Open Book" period were found and made their way into the media.

ANGELO "BIG ANGE" LONARDO

Further proof of the approval rule comes from Angelo Lonardo, a former Acting Boss of the Cleveland Family. He told a Senate committee, "In 1977, Licavoli (James Licavoli, the Cleveland Boss) and I traveled to New York

City to see Salerno (Tony Salerno, front Boss of the Genovese Family) and requested permission to 'make' 10 new members into the Cleveland Family. Salerno (on behalf of the Commission) granted our request..."

GEORGE FRESOLONE

George Fresolone was a Philadelphia mob associate based in New Jersey. His autobiography" Blood Oath" details his mob life. For our purposes, the focus will be much sharper. In a semi-secret move, Fresolone was inducted into the Philadelphia Family, on July 23, 1990.

Joseph "Scoops" Licata, a Capo, was not invited to the ceremony, Licata felt slighted and started making a fuss. He complained that a "list" had not been circulated among the New York Families, thus bringing into question the legitimacy of Fresolone's induction.

Fresolone's defense was that it was not mandatory for the Philadelphia Family to get Commission approval for inductions, but it was often done as a courtesy. The point is not who was right or wrong, but that the dispute helps prove there was a sharing of lists, at least in New York.

NICKY BIANCO

Bianco was from New England but had gravitated to New York. There, he hooked up with the violent Gallo gang, which was a crew in the Joe Profaci Family (Colombo). A shooting war broke out between Colombo factions. The violence caused a lot of publicity. Many peace efforts were made. At one point, the Gallo gang had no made members on the street for what few they had were locked up.

At this point, Bianco traveled back to Providence, Rhode Island and conferred with New England Boss Ray Patriarca. After much discussion with the Commission, Patriarca received permission to make Bianco. This allowed Bianco to represent the Gallo crew at formal sit-downs with the Colombo Family leaders.

Thanks to an illegal FBI bug in Patriarca's office, the FBI was aware of these matters, and thus they were preserved and available for use in this piece to support the Approval Rule.

THE CHICAGO OUTFIT

The Chicago Outfit is the term used to refer to the La Cosa Nostra Family in that city. It was/is merely an extension of the Capone Family from 1931. This Family, although it had a Commission seat, ran its territory as it saw fit. The Outfit rarely sought Commission approval for any action they might take. An example of an exception would have been discussions over control of the Teamsters Union.

From 1959 till the summer of 1965, the FBI had the Outfit nearly entirely covered by illegal bugs. With long-time access to this information, former FBI Agent Bill Roemer wrote that the Outfit did not conduct induction ceremonies. He was wrong.

In Jeff Coen's book on the Chicago Outfit called, "Family Secrets" he relates mobster Nick Calabrese's memory of being inducted on October 9, 1993. A gun and knife were on the table, speeches were made, and a holy card was burned, while Calabrese held it in his hand. Then a pinprick drew a few drops of blood from one of his fingers. Present at the ceremony were Boss Joey Aiuppa and most of the leaders of the Family.

This induction was a near duplicate to Valachi's version and the ceremony in New England that was taped by the FBI.

INDUCTION RULE EXCEPTION?

No evidence has emerged to indicate the Chicago Outfit sought permission from the Commission to induct members. However, we have reliable information that this rule was regularly applied in the Families east of Chicago and especially in New York City.

The next chapter will examine another function of the Commission, approving both the selection of a new Boss and the whacking of an incumbent.

CHAPTER NINE

The Commission Rules: Part Two

APPROVING THE KILLING OF A BOSS

In theory, it is accepted that the Commission had to approve the murder of a sitting Boss or one that had retired. In practice, things got a bit murky. What follows is a recitation of facts surrounding some deaths or attempted murders of sitting Bosses and retired Bosses.

DR. JOE ROMANO

Some might be surprised that Joe Romano, a medical doctor, was once Boss of a Mafia Family, but it is true. There were other "professional" people in La Cosa Nostra including a dentist (Greg Genovese, Bonanno's son-in-law) and a lawyer. (Los Angeles Boss Frank DeSimone.)

Romano was Boss of Cleveland from some unknown date till 1917 when he retired. He was replaced by Joe Lonardo, a D'Aquila favorite. Lonardo was killed, on October 13, 1927, in a coup supported by New York's Joe Masseria. Many of Lonardo's brothers were also wiped out over a period of time.

Two years later, on June 11, 1929, Angelo Lonardo, son of the slain Joe Lonardo, gunned down Sam Todaro, the new Cleveland Boss and one of the men who plotted to kill his father. Meanwhile, over the next six years, Joe Porello, the Boss who replaced Todaro, and a bunch of his brothers were slain.

In the spring of 1936, one of Angelo Lonardo's cousins had an appendix problem, and they engaged Dr. Joe Romano to operate. The cousin died. Lonardo et al. were infuriated. They had always suspected that Romano had been in on the plot to kill Joe Lonardo. Now they felt Romano had murdered their cousin. A hasty decision to kill Romano was made. This was accomplished on June 9, 1936.

All hell broke loose. Commission member Vincent Mangano, of New York's Gambino Family, was particularly upset. He probably was a personal friend of Romano. Mangano demanded the head of John DeMarco, brother of the man who died on the operating table and a cousin of Angelo Lonardo. DeMarco was on the hot seat because he was an inducted member and knew the rules. Lonardo skated for he was not made and Mangano figured he was led astray by his cousin. DeMarco went on the run.

In Angelo Lonardo's Senate testimony on April 15, 1988, he explained how the Cleveland Boss, Al Polizzi, had to travel to Miami to attend a Commission meeting. Polizzi hoped to get DeMarco's death sentenced annulled. Lonardo said he was present in the house while the Commission debated in the backyard. DeMarco was saved.

This example demonstrates that even the killing of a former Boss needs to be approved by the Commission. In the Romano case, the protocol wasn't followed. It is now appropriate to look at some other Boss killings to see if the rule came into play there.

VINCENT MANGANO

The Boss of the Gambino Family disappeared in April 1951. His body has never been found. If the Commission rule had been followed, six of the seven Commission members would have taken a vote on whether to approve this murder. (Obviously, they are not going to ask the potential victim to vote on his own fate). Since Mangano was killed, it is reasonable to presume a majority, if not all members, signed off on the hit. What little evidence we have does not support this conclusion.

When Mangano was elected Boss back in 1931, mob politics forced him to appoint Albert Anastasia as his Underboss. They were entirely different men. Mangano was calm and reasoned whereas Anastasia was referred to as the "Volcano." This was due to his ferocious temper and tendency to violence. Complicating matters was the fact that they were both powers on the Brooklyn docks. It was surprising that the "partnership lasted till 1951.

Boss Joe Bonanno claimed he was away in Arizona when he heard the news of Mangano's disappearance. Bonanno wrote that Anastasia attended a Commission meeting, but did not admit to the murder. Instead, Anastasia claimed to have proof that Mangano was plotting against him and thus he had the right to act in self-defense.

Frank Costello, Boss of the Genovese Family, supported Anastasia's story. This strongly suggested that he had been in on the conspiracy. None of the other Bosses challenged this fait accompli. The Commission then approved Anastasia as the new Boss of the Gambino Family.

Bonanno wrote that there was no vote taken to approve a hit on Mangano. Bonanno was a notorious liar and, in his autobiography, rewrote much of mob history. But, we have another first-hand account that supports his version of events. To tell that story we have to discuss Frank Scalise, who was Mangano's Consigliere.

FRANK SCALISE

In the 1920s, Scalise was a member of the Salvatore D'Aquila Family. (Gambino) We have related how Al Mineo killed D'Aquila and became the new Boss. Mineo, in an alliance with Joe Masseria, was fighting with the Maranzano forces. This enemy succeeded in killing both Mineo and his underboss, Steve Ferrigno, in 1930.

Scalise, a leading member of the Mineo group, then defected to the Maranzano camp. When Masseria was killed in April 1931, Maranzano supported Scalise's election as the new Boss of the Gambino Family.

Unfortunately for Scalise, his reign was short. Maranzano was murdered a few months after Masseria, by the Lucky Luciano crew. Now the members of the Gambino Family were anxious. They worried that they'd be out of favor with Luciano since they were being led by a Maranzano favorite. Consequently, they voted in a new Boss, Vincent Mangano. He had defected to the Maranzano camp before Scalise. To sooth Scalise's pride, Mangano appointed him Consigliere.

Now fast forward from 1931 to 1951. Boss Mangano was killed by Albert Anastasia, who became the new Boss. Anastasia was very wary of the ambitions of Scalise. The trick for Anastasia was to find a "legitimate" reason to kill Scalise, even if it was made up. Soon rumors were floating around that Scalise was selling memberships in the Family. Worse yet, he was supposedly not sharing the loot. Scalise was whacked out June 17, 1956.

Nicola Gentile, in his own 1963 autobiography, shed some light on these complicated affairs, and his version supports that of Bonanno.

Gentile described Anastasia as a loose cannon and backs up that view by claiming Anastasia whacked out Mangano without Commission approval. Anastasia then promised the Commission he'd never do that again. Oops! According to Gentile, Anastasia then had Scalise murdered without approval. (The Commission was supposed to approve hits on Underbosses and Consigliere too)

ALBERT ANASTASIA

After being in power for only six years, Anastasia died on October 25, 1957, in a spectacular, headline-grabbing hit. Was a Commission vote taken?

Gentile didn't say there was a vote, but that was clearly implied. It was Gentile who revealed that Anastasia had killed both Mangano and Scalise, without approval, thus making all the other Bosses very afraid of him. For Gentile, the Commission decided Anastasia had to go, and he did.

Bonanno, on the other hand, was fuzzy on the subject. Apparently, he did not want to publicly admit to being a part of a murder for there is no statute of limitations on that crime. Bonanno was on a trip abroad when Anastasia was killed. Upon his return to the US, Bonanno claimed he heard about the hit for the first time, "The news shocked me deeply."

Bonanno was in shock for he took credit for a peace deal between Anastasia and his chief rival, Vito Genovese, the newly elected Boss of the Family that still bears his name. In other words, Bonanno was claiming he didn't participate in any vote on Anastasia's fate. We are left with two conflicting stories, was there a vote or not?

An educated guess would be that the Commission did vote to approve a hit on Anastasia. Bonanno would have been a dissenter for he needed Anastasia's support. Knowing it was just a matter of time before Anastasia was whacked, Bonanno took an extensive trip home to Italy. It strains credulity that Bonanno did not hear of Anastasia's October demise until his return in November. He must have believed his readers didn't know there were phones in 1957!

The two examples of Mangano and Anastasia do not provide solid proof that the Commission voted on their deaths. We'll conclude that they didn't vote on Mangano but did on Anastasia. Our next example, the 1980 murder of Philadelphia Boss Angelo Bruno, a Commission member might clear up the confusion. Not!

ANGELO BRUNO

In March of 1980, Angelo Bruno had been Boss of the Philadelphia Family for more than twenty years. He was often referred to as, "The Docile Don" for his consistent laid-back style. This was due to his preference for arbitrating the inevitable disputes, rather than pulling out the guns at the first opportunity.

Bruno was very close to Carlo Gambino, the powerful Boss of the Gambino Family. Since Philadelphia was given a Commission seat in 1961, Bruno automatically became a Commission member. His alliance with Gambino gave him great strength.

Unfortunately for Bruno, Gambino died of natural causes in 1976, thus weakening Bruno somewhat. A series of prison sentences for refusing to testify before a crime inquiry further loosened his hold on power.

On March 20, 1980, Bruno was killed by a shotgun blast as he was sitting in the passenger seat of a vehicle parked outside his home. Everyone ran for cover/protection as they waited to see what would unfold. The Commission quickly became involved.

At first, everyone assumed this had to have been a Commission approved hit, especially since Bruno was a member. As time went on that theory began to appear shaky.

What was clear to everyone was that Consigliere Anthony "Tony Bananas" Caponigro was behind the murder and was perhaps even the shooter.

Philip Leonetti was a Philly hood who rose through the ranks and eventually became Underboss to Nicky Scarfo. He provided us with his version of events in his book, "Mafia Prince."

Leonetti claimed that Caponigro sought permission to kill Bruno from Frank "Funzi" Tieri, the Boss of the Genovese Family. (Tieri was actually a front Boss). Apparently, Caponigro was told that the Commission approved the hit. Delighted with this response, Caponigro had Bruno killed.

Meanwhile, Caponigro's rivals in the Family, Underboss Phil Testa, and Nicky Scarfo, checked these facts with a close contract in the Genovese Family, Consigliere Bobby Manna. He related that no permission was given by the Commission. Not long afterward, Caponigro was called to New York. He was accompanied by Alfred Salerno. They were both brutally killed because they didn't follow this Commission rule.

Leonetti believed that the Genovese Family wanted both Bruno and Caponigro eliminated. Then they could gain influence in Northern New Jersey and have a Boss on the Philadelphia throne who was owing to them. It's a complicated theory, but to date seems to be the most logical explanation of Bruno's death. However, this hit then becomes another example of a Commission rule not being followed since the Genovese Family gave the order on their own.

SAM GIANCANNA

Sam Giancanna was Boss of the Chicago Outfit from 1957 till his forced retirement in 1966. He wasn't killed until June 1975, so his case will be examined under the category of a killing of a non-sitting Boss.

Although Giancanna was the "formal" Boss of the Chicago Outfit, everyone knew that Anthony Accardo, the Consigliere, and former Boss, was the real power in that organization.

A few years after becoming Boss, Giancanna's luck changed dramatically. FBI Director Hoover ordered a no holds barred information gathering offensive against La Cosa Nostra. Giancanna was in the crosshairs. An intensive, illegal bugging operation revealed most of Giancanna's secrets to the Feds. They knew where he was going and with whom. Information was leaked to the media with the result Giancanna became a household name. The fact that he was dating Phyllis McGuire, one of the most famous singers of the time, only added to the frenzy.

Everything started going downhill for Giancanna when he was called before a federal grand jury. In a carefully planned offensive, the government pushed Giancanna into a corner by granting him immunity. That meant he could not hide behind the protection of the Fifth Amendment. Giancanna had no choice but to refuse to testify.

Giancanna was convicted of contempt and sentenced to prison on June 1, 1965. He was released at the end of May the following year, but his rule atop the Chicago Outfit was over. An 8-year odyssey in Mexico and elsewhere followed.

On July 18, 1974, the feds succeeded in convincing the Mexican government to deport Giancanna back to the United States. He returned to Chicago only to be killed in the basement of his own home on July 19, 1975

There were/are all kinds of theories as to why Giancanna was murdered. One claimed that the Chicago Outfit was angry because Giancanna was not sharing the revenues from the many casinos he had set up outside the United States.

Another idea was that the leaders of his Family feared he might talk when he appeared before the Senate Church Committee. It was examining the murky world of US intelligent operations. (Giancanna had been involved in a CIA/Mafia plot to whack Fidel Castro)

A more unlikely theory was that people feared that Giancanna might make a move to regain the Chicago throne. (That idea can be totally ignored).

This is not the place to examine these theories. For our purposes, we want to know who gave the ok to whack out the former Boss.

Everyone knew that the murder would not have happened without the approval of Anthony Accardo. He was technically the Consigliere. But Accardo was the real power. This was confirmed when Chicago Soldier Nick Calabrese began talking to the FBI in 2002. He said he knew Accardo was involved in the Giancanna hit as was Capo Angelo LaPietra. Calabrese went on to say that the .22 gun used in the murder, had a silencer which was made by his brother Frank and another man.

It is logical to conclude that Boss Joey Aiuppa and Underboss Jackie Cerone had signed off on the hit as well. That meant the entire administration of the Chicago Outfit had "approved" the murder. But what about the "Commission"?

The Chicago Outfit had a seat on the Commission from its birth back in 1931. But geography and independent power slowly changed their regular appearances to rare ones. Often they'd just send in their vote by proxy.

Evidence to support an entire Commission vote has yet to emerge. This leads us to make the reasonably confident conclusion that the Giancanna matter was handled by the Chicago Outfit alone. In fact turncoat, Cleveland Underboss, Angelo Lonardo, testified that the Chicago Outfit was a separate Commission.

FRANK COSTELLO

As we have discussed, Boss Lucky Luciano of the Genovese Family went off to prison in 1936. Underboss Vito Genovese seemed to be the logical replacement, but he got jammed up in a murder investigation and took it on the lamb to Italy in 1937. Frank Costello stepped into the breach and remained on top of the heap till 1957.

Costello then began to be undermined/challenged by Underboss Vito Genovese. Vito had been arrested in Italy in 1944 on an old murder charge. Shortly after that, he was brought back to the US. In 1946 a judge threw out the case against Genovese, and he was soon barking at the heels of a wary Costello.

On May 2, 1957, Costello was wounded by Vincent "Chin" Gigante. He immediately stepped down as Boss. At the time, Gigante was a lowly Soldier and was acting on orders. Luckily for Gigante, Costello refused to identify him as the shooter and Gigante walked. As part of the investigation, the NYPD concluded that Gigante's driver Tommy Eboli and Dom Alongi were also involved. Everyone in the mob knew this was a Genovese operation.

Bonanno isn't helpful to us on this matter. He stated that both rivals, Vito Genovese and Albert Anastasia, had been attempting to shore up their power.

They did so by developing alliances with other mob leaders. But Bonanno does not say a vote was taken to approve a hit on Costello.

Years later, Buffalo Boss Stefano Magaddino was taped saying that he was not told that Costello was going to be hit. Magaddino went on to claim that some other Commission members insisted he had been told by another person. When that other person was contacted, he said that not only didn't he tell Magaddino that a hit on Costello was approved, but that he didn't know himself. (It is unclear if this mysterious person is another Commission member).

CONCLUSION

It has been widely accepted that a Boss (or Underboss or Consigliere) couldn't be killed unless the Commission approved it. Unfortunately, the evidence is mixed on the truth of this claim. The rule seems to exist, but the problem is whether it was applied or not in each particular hit.

CHAPTER TEN

The Commission Rules: Part Three

PROOF THAT THE COMMISSION
APPROVES ALL NEW BOSSES

Approval of new Bosses was a logical rule for the Commission to have. No one wanted some renegade who was going to cause problems. Secondly, in theory, it was a means to prevent a fellow Commission member from stacking the deck with allies, to control the Commission. Below are examples which show Commission oversight on the elevation of new Bosses.

GREG SCARPA

Colombo Soldier (briefly a Capo) Greg Scarpa started informing to the FBI early in 1961. His Boss, Joe Profaci, died the following year and Scarpa updated the agents that Joe Magliocco was going to be the new leader and that his name would be submitted to the Commission for approval.

ANGELO BRUNO

On November 14, 1957, New York State Troopers stumbled on a National Meeting near Apalachin, New York, which is close to the Pennsylvania border. Joe Ida, the Philadelphia Family Boss, was briefly detained and identified, then released. Headline stories across the nation included his name. He wanted out of LCN immediately. By 1959, Ida had permanently returned to Italy.

Dominick Pollina was appointed Acting Boss, but he was quickly caught plotting to kill Capo Angelo Bruno, a rival. The Commission voted Pollina out, and suddenly Bruno was the new Boss.

An FBI bug in the office of Sam Decavalcante, Boss of the New Jersey Family, revealed that Bruno was on probation for three years before finally being confirmed as the official Boss of the Philadelphia Family by the Commission.

PHIL TESTA

As described in the previous chapter, Angelo Bruno was killed on March 21, 1980. The Commission immediately became involved in the investigation of his death. Heads rolled. Then the Commission ordered Underboss Phil Testa to New York.

From former Philadelphia Underboss Phil Leonetti, we learned what happened at this meeting. Vincent "Chin" Gigante, the Genovese Boss, "... tells Phil Testa that the Commission had decided that he is now the Boss of the Philadelphia mob..."

A few days later at a gathering of all the Philadelphia Capos, Testa announced his selection for Underboss and Consigliere. Present at the meeting was Bobby Manna, the Genovese Consigliere. His presence indicated that the Commission had approved of Testa becoming Boss.

NICKY SCARFO

On March 15, 1981, Testa was blown apart by a bomb hidden under his front porch. Once again the Commission stepped in and heads rolled.

Consigliere Nicky Scarfo knew he was in an excellent position to be the new king. He was tight with Bobby Manna, the Genovese Consigliere, and had the support of many Philadelphia Capos. Nevertheless, there was the outside possibility Underboss Peter Casella would be anointed. That idea quickly evaporated when Scarfo and Casella sat down in front of the Genovese administration, which was representing the Commission.

Surprisingly, Casella admitted plotting Testa's murder and named his co-conspirators. Gigante then ordered Casella to leave Philadelphia immediately and never return. After Casella departed the room, Gigante turned to Scarfo and said, "Well, Nick, I don't see no one else here, so I guess that makes you the new Boss."

What a mistake! Scarfo would then lead the Family into decades of turmoil and violence. That is another story. For our purposes, the point is that it was the Genovese Family, with the backing of the Commission, which not only approved a new Boss but actually appointed him.

JACK LICAVOLI

Angelo Lonardo, a former Underboss/Acting Boss of the Cleveland Family, testified before a Senate Committee about our next example.

Cleveland Boss John Scalish died of natural causes in 1976. According to his brother-in-law, Milton "Maishe" Rockman, an influential Associate, Scalish wanted Capo Jack Licavoli to replace him. That was done, and Licavoli selected his Underboss and Consigliere. It is interesting that there was no mention of a vote by the Capos to formalize this new regime.

Lonardo went on to testify that, "One day, I asked Licavoli if he had gone to New York and introduced himself to Tony Salerno as boss of the Family." Licavoli replied in the negative, so Lonardo explained that the Genovese Family represented Cleveland's interest on the Commission. He said it was only right that Licavoli go to New York to see Salerno. Lonardo reported that this was done. In so many words, Lonardo was confirming that a new Boss had to be approved by the Commission.

JOHN LAROCCA

LaRocca was Boss of the Pittsburgh Family from 1957 till his death on December 3, 1984.

The 1980 Pennsylvania Crime Commission Report explained why it was necessary for the Family to pick a new Boss to replace Frank Amato. The document said, "In 1956, Amato developed an acute kidney ailment and resigned..." LaRocca became the new Boss. It is assumed that the Capos voted on LaRocca's elevation.

On September 21, 1964, a bug in the office of Sam Decavalcante, Boss of the New Jersey Family, heard Decavalcante say, "They made LaRocca take orders from the Commission until everything was straightened out." The Commission kept LaRocca on probation for about three years before finally giving him their final blessing. This example is further proof that the Commission was involved in approving new Bosses.

MATTHEW "MIKE" TRUPIANO and ANTHONY PARINO

Trupiano was the St. Louis Boss from 1980 till his natural death in 1997. He was replaced by long-time Consigliere, Anthony Parino who endured until 2014. The details of their lives leading the rapidly declining St. Louis Family are not necessary at this time.

FBI reports indicated that when Trupiano was to become Boss, a meeting was held, in Chicago, to discuss whether to approve his elevation. At that gathering were; Joey Aiuppa, the Boss of Chicago, Anthony Accardo, the Chicago Consigliere, and Detroit Boss Jack Tocco. They must have signed off on Trupiano for he took the leadership position and held it for many years.

A similar situation arose when Parino became Boss. The FBI monitored a meeting between; Boss Jack Tocco of Detroit, his Capo, Anthony Corrado, Chicago Boss John DiFronzo, and Chicago Consigliere, Joey Lombardo.

Chicago and Detroit were approving the new Bosses in St. Louis, not the Commission. It's true that Chicago had a seat on the Commission but Detroit did not during these changes in leadership.

CONCLUSION

From our examples, it is clear that the LCN rules required that each new Boss must be approved by the Commission. As time passed and our knowledge of La Cosa Nostra grew, it emerged that Chicago was acting as a Commission for the Families in Middle America and the far west. A new Boss in these areas had to be approved, not by the Commission, but by Chicago alone. No matter, a new Boss had to be approved by "higher" authority. It appears that this rule was regularly respected although we do not have evidence about the elevation of many Bosses from smaller Families.

CHAPTER ELEVEN

The Commission Rules: Part Four

NO NARCOTICS!

This chapter is not a history of drug laws in the United States nor of the various efforts that the government has made to curtail the illegal use of drugs. Our purpose is to examine whether there is evidence that a Commission ban on drug dealing existed, and if it did, how effective was it?

It is widely accepted that the Commission banned members of La Cosa Nostra from being involved with drugs. The Bosses' reasoning was simple. The public, the police, and the politicians viewed the sale and use of drugs as despicable. This response was entirely different than their laissez-faire attitude towards alcohol and gambling. The Bosses feared that a great outcry about drugs would force the politicians and police to crack down, thus disrupting all their other rackets, many of which operated under "protection." Also, they feared that the penalties for drug dealing, which were regularly being increased, would tempt those caught to turn informer. This rule made sense, but as Joe Valachi testified, "Because of the money-making, the profit in it, they would chance their own lives."

PROOF OF THE DRUG BAN

There is primary evidence of the existence of the drug ban from the testimony of La Cosa Nostra members who became informants. Below is a sampling of some of this material.

JOE VALACHI

When Valachi testified before a Senate Committee in October of 1963, he gave us some excellent information on the ban. According to Valachi, his Boss, Frank Costello barred all Genovese Family members from dealing in drugs. This was in 1948. Valachi went on to explain that the other four New York Families did not have this prohibition and thus could make a lot of money dealing narcotics.

Valachi said that Albert Anastasia, the Underboss, then later Boss of the Gambino Family, was heavily into drugs and just would not discuss a comprehensive ban. Presumably, Valachi was telling us that Anastasia's refusal prevented the Commission from imposing an injunction. This interpretation is supported when Valachi said, "After Anastasia died in 1957, all Families were notified—no narcotics."

JOE BONANNO

In his autobiography, "Joe Bonanno, Man of Honor" Bonanno wrote, "My tradition outlaws narcotics." Fully aware that many of his members, including his handpicked Underboss, Carmine Galante, were convicted of drug dealing, Bonanno tried to cover himself. He also wrote, "The lure of high profits had tempted some underlings to freelance in the narcotics trade."

SAMMY "SAMMY the BULL" GRAVANO

Gravano is one of the most famous mob turncoats of all time. He was the Underboss in the Gambino Family under Boss John Gotti. Sammy got jammed up on severe charges and rolled over to prevent spending the rest of his life in the slammer. Later Peter Maas wrote Gravano's autobiography "Underboss." In it, Gravano is quoted as saying, "Death was the penalty for anyone in the Family dealing drugs."(It's ironic that Gravano blew his incredibly lenient witness deal by dealing drugs and ending up in prison doing a long sentence.)

JOHN GOTTI

In the book, "Gotti, Rise and Fall," the authors, Jerry Capeci and Gene Mustain, quoted information from a Gambino Family Associate about the ban. The informer said, "Carló (Gambino, the Boss of the Family) had also told Gotti to re-emphasize the ban on drug dealing." (Gotti and his buddies were up to their necks in dealing heroin)

MICHAEL FRANZESE

Franzese rose to be a Capo in the Colombo Family based on the fact he was bringing in tens of millions from a gasoline scam. The fact that he was the son of the legendary Sonny Franzese wouldn't have hurt either. Eventually, Franzese got jammed up on serious charges and did unpleasant time in the slammer. In a fantastic move, he "retired" from the mob, and has spent his life spreading the word of the Gospel through the story of his life.

In his autobiography, "Quitting the Mob," Franzese wrote about his induction. Boss (or more likely Acting Boss) Tom DiBella told him, "never become involved in illegal narcotics."

PHIL "CRAZY PHIL" LEONETTI

Leonetti, at one time, was the Underboss of the Philadelphia Family. After being convicted and given a very long prison sentence, he rolled over and became a protected witness. Like most of these famous turncoats, Leonetti also wrote his autobiography called, "Mafia Prince." He wrote that "Dealing drugs was an absolute violation of the rules!"

PAUL CASTELLANO

Unlike many of the above examples, Paul Castellano, Boss of the Gambino Family, did not live long enough to write his autobiography. However, we know his take on the embargo from his own words. They were captured on hidden FBI bugs in his Staten Island Mansion. Two FBI agents, Joe O'Brien and Andris Kurins, wrote an excellent book called, "Boss of Bosses" in which they told of the fall of Castellano. They summed up Castellano's view of the ban this way, "No one caught dealing drugs after 1962 could become an initiated member of the Gambino Family." They went on to say that any present member would be whacked if caught dealing drugs.

ANTHONY ACCARDO

Accardo ruled the Chicago Outfit, mostly from the Consigliere position, from 1931 till around 1989. In the book, "Accardo" by long-time FBI agent Bill Roemer, the agent addressed the embargo, "All throughout Tony Accardo's reign in Chicago, the Outfit prohibited its members from having any involvement whatsoever in the drug business."

Valachi's 1963 testimony before the Senate Committee supported Roemer. Valachi explained that Chicago was paying $200 a week to those of its soldiers who were involved in the drug trade before the ban as a means of compensation for their lost income. (The difficulty of carrying out that policy suggests it never happened)

CONCLUSION

The evidence seems airtight that a Commission moratorium on drug dealing was in place after 1957. Jimmy Fratianno, in his autobiography, "The Last Mafioso" claims that at his induction into the Los Angeles Family, in 1947, he was told, "You must never become involved with narcotics." As stated above, Bonanno said that his Tradition banned narcotics. We know his "Tradition" goes way back into the late 1880s, so it is reasonable to conclude that the drug ban goes back at least to the 1931 birth of the Commission.

WAS THE DEATH PENALTY APPLIED?

Theoretically, any inducted member of an LCN Family would be put to death if convicted of drug dealing. ESPECIALLY if his activities jammed up other members. A few examples will be discussed below.

The following account is from Bill Roemer's excellent book, "Accardo."

CHRIS CARDI

Chris Cardi was a Chicago Outfit Associate whose uncle was a respected Soldier. Cardi bounced around from the police department to loan shark debt collecting and then into drugs. Things went south fast after that.

First of all, the Outfit had a ban on drug dealing. Secondly, the publicity of Cardi's arrest and trial would bring lousy PR down on the heads of the Outfit because of Cardi's connection to his inducted uncle. Finally, Anthony Accardo, the all-powerful Consigliere, just could not let anyone believe he wasn't going to have this rule followed to the letter. Cardi was a goner long before he knew it.

Roemer claimed that the Outfit devised a diabolical plan to deal with Cardi. Using their Soldier, Pat Marcy, who dominated Chicago politics in the First Ward, a "compliant" judge was picked to hear the case. His job was to make sure Cardi was convicted AND given a long sentence. Both of those things happened, but Roemer's account is the only evidence to support its truth.

In any event, Cardi was released from prison, only to be gunned down, on June 19, 1975, in front of his wife and three kids. Accardo was indeed sending a crystal clear message about the seriousness of the no drug rule.

JOE DEMACA

In his 1963 Senate testimony, Valachi was speaking about what happened to those who got caught violating the drug ban. He said, "A few got caught, and they paid with their lives." He then mentioned the name "Joe DeMaca" as being one of the victims.

ANTHONY "THE GAWK" AUGELLO

Augello was a veteran Soldier in the Colombo Family. In the early 1980's, he got jammed up in a drug case that also involved, Alphonse "Alley Boy" Persico Jr., son of Boss Carmine Persico. According to Michael Franzese, Augello was beside himself with fright, figuring it was only a matter of time before Boss Carmine Persico sent a hit team after him.

On May 9, 1983, Augello used a .357 magnum to blow his brains out. Franzese wrote, "The drug case against the younger Persico... was dropped. The Gawk hit himself for nothing." This was a self-imposed death penalty for breaking the Commission's rule against drug dealing.

PETER "LITTLE PETE" TAMBONE

In 1956, Tambone was given a five-year drug sentence. By the 1980s, he was on the fringes of the John Gotti crew and still dealing heroin. Word got back to Boss Paul Castellano, who was livid. He pronounced a death sentence on Tambone, probably more to send a message to the Gotti crew than to punish Tambone himself.

Gotti's buddy, Angelo Ruggiero, started a frantic campaign to save Tambone. The real reason for his efforts was not so much to save Little Pete's hide but to prevent Ruggiero's own drug dealing from becoming clear to Castellano.

Ruggiero begged his Underboss, Aniello "Neil" Dellacroce, to save Tambone. Thanks to a bug in Ruggiero's home, he was heard retelling his conversation with Dellacroce. "...I give you my word this, he won't see nobody no more, and he won't bother with nobody no more." Ruggiero then said that Dellacroce accepted this mild punishment and that Boss Paul Castellano would go along with it too. Tambone was "banished" from LCN, but at least he wasn't dead.

SURVIVING THE BAN

If the Commission ban on drugs is valid, it follows that members who were convicted of drug dealing would never rise in the Family. That is not the case with the following LCN members.

JOSEPH "JOE PINEY" ARMONE

He did time on a narcotics conviction yet rose to be a Capo in the Gambino Family. He moved up to Underboss and Consigliere in the Gotti era.

ALFRED "AL WALKER" EMBARRATO

This Bonanno Family member spent time in prison on a drug violation, but he was later promoted to Capo in the 1970s.

NATALE "JOE DIAMOND" EVOLA

Despite a drug conviction, the Bonanno Capo was elected Boss of the Family in 1970 and reigned for 3 years. Back in the 1930s, he was in Joe Bonanno's wedding party.

CARMINE "LILO" GALANTE

He was the Bonanno Family Underboss when he was convicted of a narcotics conspiracy. After doing his time, he muscled his way to the top and spent a few years as the unofficial Boss.

VINCENT "CHIN" GIGANTE

In the early sixties, Gigante did time for a drug violation, yet rose to be Boss of the Genovese Family in 1981.

PHILIP "COCKEYED PHIL" LOMBARDO

Despite two Federal Narcotics convictions, Lombardo became a long time "hidden" Boss of the Genovese Family, in the 1970s.

ANTHONY "TONY" MIRRA

This Bonanno Soldier became famous due to his contacts with FBI undercover agent Joe Pistone. Mira had a narcotics conviction on his record but was able to return to the Bonanno Family upon his release from prison.

JOHN "BIG JOHN" ORMENTO

Despite three narcotics convictions, Ormento was able to operate as a Lucchese Family Capo before yet another drug sentence.

SALVATORE "SAM" PIERI

When Pieri was the Buffalo Family Underboss, he was convicted of a drug conspiracy and began a ten-year sentence on August 31, 1956. Pieri was released seven years later. He started a long, slow climb to the top of the Family. Pieri became Boss in 1974.

SALVATORE "TOM MIX" SANTORO

Santoro was a defendant in the 1986 Commission trial. At the time, he was the Underboss of the Lucchese Family despite having two narcotics law convictions.

CONCLUSION

The evidence shows there was a ban on drug dealing and some paid the extreme penalty for violating the rule. However, our list of those who thrived after a drug conviction clearly demonstrates the law was ineffective. It is impossible to evaluate whether the fear of punishment kept a lot of other LCN members out of the drug trade.

CHAPTER TWELVE

The Commission Rules: Part Five

OMERTA

(Keep your mouth shut)

If you are a member or an Associate of La Cosa Nostra, it's inevitable you'll be doing some illegal stuff at some point in time. If there was a rule that forbad any of your companions from telling the cops about the crime, you'd be in a pretty secure position, especially before DNA.

It isn't surprising then, that at the beginning of the Mafia, the rule against talking, Omerta, was strictly enforced. Just the fear of the retribution that would come down on your head if you spoke prevented many from informing, let alone testifying in court. This rule kept many Mafia members out of prison. Around the time of the Commission case, that rule was falling apart with dire consequences for LCN members.

What follows are accounts of some poor souls who fell victim to this rule. Then we will look at those who survived thanks to the Witness Security Program. (WITSEC)

VICTIMS OF THE RULE

CARLO CARRAMUSA

In February of 1942, a search of the Kansas City home of Fellipo Pernice uncovered a hidden stash of drugs. Pernice was arrested and charged along with; Paul and Joe Antinori, Joe DeLuca, James Desimone, and Carl Carramusa. The Antinoris were running a sophisticated drug ring which obtained heroin manufactured in Marseilles France. The drug was transported to Cuba then smuggled into the Tampa Bay, Florida area. From there it was moved to Chicago, Kansas City, and other locations in the Midwest. The Antinoris' father was in charge of the operation and was a significant crime operator. Unfortunately for the elder Antinoris, a gunman blew him away in 1940, leaving the two sons to carry on.

A year after the arrests, Carramusa was convicted and sentenced to four years. Surprisingly, he quickly rolled over and agreed to testify against his partners. In March of 1943, Carramusa was a witness as the five listed above were convicted and sentenced to a variety of terms, from time served/probation to seven years. Carramusa then went into hiding in Chicago.

That plan didn't work too well. Even though Carramusa knew that people were following him, he didn't immediately flee. He was running a store and had a family to support. On June 21, 1945, Carramusa drove to his home at 837 Lawndale Avenue. His daughter was standing on the porch with two friends when a black vehicle roared up, and three shotgun blasts tore into Carramusa. Not surprisingly, he was dead.

EUGENIO GIANNINI

Giannini was a young, bounce around hood who was recruited into the Lucchese Family, along with Joe Valachi and others. They were needed to beef up the regime, as it fought against the dictates of Joe Masseria, in the Castellammarese War. Afterward, Giannini didn't distinguish himself but managed to make a living being involved in a variety of rackets.

At some point, Giannini became an informant for the Bureau of Narcotics, (BN) (a forerunner of today's Drug Enforcement Agency-DEA). That was confirmed by the November 14, 1952 testimony of George White, the Bureau of Narcotics supervisor for New England. White was appearing before the New York State Crime Commission. He said that Giannini had supplied details of the organization of the Lucchese Family and other matters. Giannini was a BN informer and thus subject to the death penalty for breaking the Commission rule.

In Valachi's testimony, before a Senate Committee, in early October 1963, he completed the story. In summary, his Capo, Tony Bender, informed him that Lucky Luciano had sent word from Italy, that Giannini was an informer. Underboss Vito Genovese then ordered Bender to have Giannini killed. There were some problems, so Valachi volunteered to arrange the hit himself. He did so for everyone knew Giannini owed Valachi money. Valachi didn't want there to be any suspicion that he was helping Giannini hide so that he could receive his loan payback.

After some false starts, the three hoods, whom Valachi had recruited to do the hit, succeeded in killing Giannini, on September 20, 1952. He was a victim because he violated the Omerta rule.

JOSEPH "THE ANIMAL" BARBOZA

Barboza was a non-Italian mobster who was much feared by those near him. From the late fifties through the mid-sixties, Barboza was on a rampage, committing a variety of crimes. Occasionally, he would get hooked up with LCN members and Associates, who were part of the Family headed by Boss Raymond Patriarca and Underboss Harry Tameleo. Also in the picture was gambling czar and Capo Jerry Anguilo, who was based in Boston. (Patriarca was in Providence, Rhode Island)

It would take a room full of books to just scratch the surface of what unfolded in the world of LCN in New England from 1960 to the present day. For those of you who are very interested in these matters I recommend "Black Mass" by Dick Lehr and Gerard O'Neil. There are other good books on the subject as well. What follows is an extremely brief summary of events that led Barboza to become an informant and thus a violator of the Omerta rule.

Barboza received permission, from Patriarca, to kill two men. (Ted Deegan and Willie Marfeo). He participated in those murders. Later, Barboza got jammed up on other charges and was incarcerated. Frustrated, Barboza started threatening to roll over, unless Patriarca et al. obtained his release. When three of his buddies were killed, by Patriarca men, Barboza did the unthinkable and started talking.

Patriarca and Tameleo were arrested. Ultimately they went to the slammer on a variety of charges with Barboza as a key prosecution witness. Sadly, Tameleo and three other innocent men were framed for murder. It was a conspiracy run by corrupt FBI agent Paul Rico. Barboza agreed to give false testimony, and the four innocents were sentenced to death. (Their death sentences were reduced to life on appeal)

In 1969, Barboza was rewarded with an early release. He eventually moved to San Francisco. Not surprisingly, Barboza got into a dispute with a man and killed him. With the help of his FBI friends, Barboza pleaded guilty to second degree murder and was only sentenced to five years. For some that was not justice. But Mafia-style retribution came down on his head on February 11, 1976. Barboza was blown away by shotgun blasts. When his Boston lawyer, F. Lee Bailey was asked for a comment, he said, "This is no great loss for society."

GEORGE FRANCONERO JR.

This young lawyer slowly got himself entangled with schemes involving officials of Local 945 of the Teamsters. Being from New Jersey and intelligent, he should have been well aware of the dangers of working with a Teamsters local, a goldmine for La Cosa Nostra. The temptation must have been too great, and soon he was in very deep.

Eventually, Franconero was facing a 2-5 year term for land fraud. Being comfortable in his middle-class life, Franconero decided to become a witness.

Franconero testified before the New Jersey State Commission of Investigations which was looking into organized crime links to union dental plans. He was also a witness in a Federal investigation into bank fraud. Franconero was in violation of the Commission Omerta rule. It applied to him, for by his activities, he had become a mob Associate.

Surprisingly, Franconero turned down an FBI offer of protection. Perhaps he didn't want to upset his comfortable daily routine. Maybe Franconero had been suckered by assurances from his mob friends that he was in no danger. In any case, two men came calling when Franconero was scraping ice off his windshield on March 6, 1981. His life was over quickly. His famous sister, singer Connie Francis, was devastated.

PETER LATEMPA

Back in 1934, LaTempa was a Genovese Family Associate who had the misfortune of being witness to Capo Mike Miranda asking Ernie "The Hawk" Rupolo to set up two men. The targets had gotten on the wrong side of Underboss Vito Genovese. The Hawk refused to lure the men to their deaths but offered to do the killings himself. For this, Miranda had to check with Genovese, so another meeting was arranged.

Rupolo met Genovese, who agreed to give Rupolo the contract on Ernie Gallo. Two other associates would whack out Ferdinand "The Shadow" Boccia. On September 19, 1934, Boccia was killed. Rupolo, as was his usual practice, blew the Gallo hit. The victim was only wounded and fingered Rupolo and another man as his assailants. Apparently, this made Genovese et al. very nervous. LaTempa may have said a few words to the good guys around about this time.

Many accounts have Genovese fleeing to Italy shortly after the Boccia hit. They are incorrect. Genovese was front and center when he was naturalized on November 25, 1936. However, on May 11, 1937, Boccia's body finally surfaced from its resting place in the Hudson River. Not too long afterward Genovese took it on the lamb to Italy.

Sad sack Rupolo had to do time on the attempted murder of Willie Gallo. He was released only to be arrested again after he blew another killing. In June of 1944, not wanting to do any more time, Rupolo made a deal with the New York prosecutors. Among other things, he told of being hired by Miranda and Genovese to commit murder.

This news hit the street quickly. A panicked Peter LaTempa rushed to the police. He was put into protective custody, in a civil prison, as a material witness. LaTempa was a wreck. Things got worse on August 6, 1944, when a grand jury indicted Genovese, Miranda, and others on the Boccia murder.

By coincidence, over in Italy, Genovese was detained for black market scams. The arresting officer checked his background and discovered that there was a warrant out for Genovese on the Boccia hit. Now Genovese was in big trouble.

News of Genovese's capture got back to LaTempa in New York. On December 6, 1944, LaTempa tried to hang himself in his cell but survived. On January 15, 1944, LaTempa was allowed an escorted walk outside the prison. He made a stop at a pharmacy and purchased some items. That same day, a brother visited him in his cell. The next morning LaTempa was found dead.

From then to the present, accounts of his death claim he was poisoned by the Mafia to protect Genovese et al. These stories are totally incorrect. A report from New York City toxicologist, Dr. Alexander Gettler, stated that LaTempa died of an overdose of sleeping pills—not poison.

LaTempa had probably been hoarding the sleeping pills that he was prescribed. He may have gotten more from his visiting brother, and he purchased some in the drugstore the day before he died. Additionally, LaTempa had attempted suicide, back in December. The evidence is clear that LaTempa took himself out. There was no elaborate Mafia plot to do him in.

Genovese arrived back in the USA on June 1, 1945. He spent the next year in prison awaiting his trial. The Hawk testified and gave a good account of his interaction with Genovese and Miranda. But with LaTempa dead, there was no collaboration of Rupolo's story. In New York State, at the time, no one could be convicted on the testimony of a participant in the crime, unless there were other witnesses. There were none, so the judge ordered the jury to find Genovese not guilty.

LaTempa had imposed the Commission penalty on himself, based on fear. The Commission Indictment of 1985 charged that the Commission imposed its will by using fear and violence. The LaTempa suicide supports that charge.

CONCLUSION

The Commission Omerta rule that if you talked, you got killed, was real and bodies were lying in the street to prove it. However, some broke the rule and lived to tell about it. Their stories are next.

DODGING BULLETS

The key to saving witnesses against the mob was the passage, in 1970, of the Organized Crime Control Act. In Title V, the details of a witness protection program were outlined. No longer would witnesses be protected by ad-hoc means or none at all. The United States finally had a formal program. It started slowly, there were mistakes made and lessons learned. However, this feature was one of the critical elements in decimating LCN. We will begin with an early turncoat whose experiences as a witness helped create the program.

Note:
I recommend, WITSEC: Inside the Federal Witness Protection Program" by Pete Early and Gerald Shur for those interested in a detailed account of the program.

PASCAL "PADDY" CALABRESE

Calabrese was a Soldier in the Buffalo Family controlled by Boss Stefano Magaddino, a Commission member. His Underboss was Fred Randaccio, and Pasquale Natarelli was a powerful Capo.

Calabrese got jammed up on a daring robbery and was doing time in the slammer. This was frustrating in itself, but Calabrese became extremely angry that the Family was not supporting his girlfriend and family, while he was unable to earn money. Calabrese complained to a Buffalo policeman who brought the problem to a member of the Federal Strike Force that was headquartered in Buffalo. They jumped at the chance to have Calabrese as a witness.

Naturally, Calabrese had many demands, before he would formally roll over. This was before WITSEC so a vague plan was hammered together and Calabrese, on February 27, 1967, joined the good guys. His testimony was vital in gaining convictions against Underboss Randaccio and Capo Natarelli. They were sent away for twenty years.

JIMMY "THE WEASEL" FRATIANNO

Jimmy "The Weasel" Fratianno is certainly one of the most famous turncoats in La Cosa Nostra history. Not only did he appear as a prosecution witness in many high profile trials, but he also figured prominently in many documentaries on the mob. Throw in the great success of his biography "The Last Mafioso" by Ovid Demaris, and the follow-up, "Vengeance is Mine" by Michael Zuckerman, and you have a "Star."

Fratianno was probably hyper from the time he was born. Starting out in Cleveland, in low-level rackets, he bounced out to LA. Eventually, connections helped him become inducted, into that Family, in 1947. It wasn't long before he was killing people on behalf of his Boss, but reaping little financial reward. The Weasel's life was basically a headlong race to gain recognition, power, and money. He achieved the former but struck out on the other two goals.

At one point, feeling unappreciated by the Los Angeles leaders, Fratianno secured a transfer to the Chicago Outfit. Again the big payday proved elusive. When the LA Boss and Underboss were on their way to prison, in 1975, they asked Capo Louis Tom Dragna to be the Acting Boss. Dragna agreed as long as he was allowed to bring Fratianno onto the team. This was acceptable to Boss Dominic Brooklier, for he was hoping Fratianno would generate money by using his fearsome reputation.

Fratianno received permission from Chicago to transfer back to the Los Angeles Family. Soon Fratianno was bouncing around the country, meeting with other LCN leaders. He often presented himself as the Acting Boss. It wasn't long before Fratianno was failing to mention "Acting." In fact, the Weasel was nothing but a Soldier who Dragna brought into his circle for intimidation purposes. For the longest time, Dragna had no idea of the many charades Fratianno was pulling. For Fratianno, this was his last chance to make big bucks.

Within two years, the whole charade had come crashing down on Fratianno's head. The leaders of the LA Family were inundated with stories of Fratianno's masquerade. They wanted him hit. To support their charges, Brooklier et al. claimed Fratianno was also trying to set up his own Family in San Francisco. Also, the FBI was preparing to charge him with participating in a Cleveland murder. The Weasel was trapped in a box.

With no money, no friends, and nowhere to run, Fratianno went into the Witness Protection Program kicking and screaming. Till the time of his death, he drove WITSEC officials crazy with his continually changing and escalating demands. Fratianno got away with it because he was an essential witness in trials in Los Angeles, Kansas City, Cleveland, and New York. As you can imagine, Fratianno demanded payment for every appearance.

On June 30, 1993, after a long battle with Alzheimer disease, the Weasel passed away. No one was ever able to impose the Commission penalty for violating Omerta on this colorful, but deadly LCN member.

CONCLUSION

As the feds began to get their ducks in order on how to run WITSEC, the word spread quickly. Everyone in the underworld knew that there was an alternative to getting killed, if you talked. Soon the government was inundated with criminals seeking protection. Among them were many LCN members and Associates. Even Boss Joe Massino of the Bonanno Family signed on. The Commission rule about Omerta was still standing, but it was a façade. Everyone in the life recognized that their "friends" would make a run for the program if things got too hot.

CHAPTER THIRTEEN

Apalachin

LA COSA NOSTRA MEETS

In the Commission Indictment, the government wanted to explain the history of the Commission, to give the jurors a better understanding of it. One of the critical events in Commission history was the discovery of a meeting of most of the Bosses of La Cosa Nostra, on November 14, 1957. An examination of that historic event follows.

THE BARBARA ESTATE

The Barbara estate was/is located at 625 McFall Road near the small town of Apalachin, New York. In November of 1957, you could see the residence from the bottom of the hill. This would prove to be significant. Also of importance was the fact that McFall Road was a dead end due to the collapse of a bridge west of the estate.

The beautiful fieldstone home was situated on 58 acres of a combination of open land and forest. It had 11 rooms, including a 1,600 square foot, living room with beautiful pine paneling on the walls. The detached four car garage was constructed of matching fieldstone. In the rear of the garage was a bar, a kitchen, and showers. Just outside was a huge BBQ in the same fieldstone. Also on the property was a summer house, a guest house, and a 12 horse stable. Even today the estate is impressive although overshadowed by the monster homes of today's top celebrities.

NATIONAL MEETINGS

After Salvatore Maranzano was killed, in September of 1931, the leaders of all the La Cosa Nostra Families met in Chicago. Joe Bonanno referred to this as the first National Meeting of La Cosa Nostra. At this gathering, the Commission was formed and the seven original members selected. It was also decided that the members would serve five-year terms. At that point, another National Meeting of La Cosa Nostra Bosses would be held. Its primary purpose would be to select seven Bosses to sit on the Commission. In reality, this was a rubber stamping operation, as whoever was then a Boss of one of the five New York Families got a seat. The same was true for Chicago and Buffalo.

A change happened in 1956. After complaints, it was decided to increase the membership of the Commission, to widen its influence and legitimacy. The Bosses of the Philadelphia and Detroit Family would have a Commission seat starting in 1961, thus moving its membership up to nine.

According to Bonanno, National Meetings were held in; 1931, 1936, 1941, 1946, 1951, and 1956. Then came the emergency, out of sequence, National Meeting, in Apalachin in 1957, and everything changed forever. It would be the last National Meeting of La Cosa Nostra.

WHY AN OUT OF SEQUENCE NATIONAL MEETING?

There have been all kinds of theories as to why the mob gathered at Apalachin in November of 1957. There is no need to discuss them. The reason for the meeting is very clear if you know La Cosa Nostra history. First, we have to look at some of the notable personalities.

VITO GENOVESE

As we've discussed earlier, Genovese fled to Italy, in 1937, to avoid a murder investigation. He was returned to the US in 1945, and his murder case was thrown out of court in 1946. Genovese was ready to assume his proper place in the Genovese Family. To Vito, that place was Boss.

Unfortunately for Genovese, Frank Costello had taken the top position, back in the 1930's, when Lucky Luciano was sent off to prison, and Genovese fled to Italy. Costello was still Boss when Genovese returned, and he showed no signs of willingness to step aside. Besides, Costello had appointed his relative, Willie Moretti, as his Underboss. Genovese had his work cut out if he wanted to sit on the throne.

WILLIE MORETTI

According to Joe Bonanno, Frank Costello began to grow closer to Albert Anastasia around this time. Costello supported Anastasia's claim of self-defense when Gambino Boss Vincent Mangano went missing in 1951. Anastasia became the new Boss, and he grew tighter with Costello.

Moretti was not pleased with this new state of affairs. He began to complain about it openly. Moretti claimed, contrary to what Costello told the Commission, that he was not aware of any plotting by Mangano to hit Anastasia. Costello must have been enraged by this criticism from his Underboss. Costello now had to come up with an "excuse" to justify whacking out the popular Moretti.

By nature, Moretti had an outgoing personality, and indeed, his dominant position did nothing to hinder his tendency to be outspoken. When he appeared before the Kefauver Committee, in 1950, he was a sensation. Rather than refusing to testify, like all the other LCN members, Moretti joked and played to the audience. This did not go over well within the Mafia, but it played right into Costello's hands.

Soon rumors were floating around saying that Moretti was sick, that his brain had been damaged by syphilis, just like Al Capone. In 1983, even Joe Bonanno wrote of Moretti, "He was in the later stages of syphilis… Willie's mind was rapidly disintegrating. He was an embarrassment."

Valachi, in his Senate testimony, confirmed this commonly held belief in fractured English. He testified that "…with Willie Moretti, as long as they made it official that he was sick that you could say was by 'commissione'. It means they all agreed."

Moretti was killed on October 4, 1951.

Approximately a decade later, Buffalo Boss Stefano Magaddino was overheard relating that after the Moretti hit, Costello was angry because Magaddino hadn't called him with his congratulations.

The problem with Bonanno's account and countless others on Moretti was that they were all wrong. Bergin County Medical Examiner Dr. Ralph

Gilady did the autopsy on Moretti. There were NO signs of brain damage. That fact has been overlooked for over sixty years.

Stefano Magaddino had it right. On October 15, 1964, Magaddino was secretly taped saying" Frank Costello killed him (Mangano) and Dellamora (Moretti) too. He went on to say this about Moretti, "He was not crazy."

In the end, the calculated move, by Costello and Anastasia, to remove the troublesome Moretti, ended up backfiring. There was no way Costello could not appoint the powerful Vito Genovese as the new Underboss. Vito must have been thinking, "One more to go."

FRANK COSTELLO

Fearing Genovese, Costello formed an alliance with Anastasia of the Gambino Family. In a roundabout way, as we discussed above, that led to the appointment of Genovese as the Family's Underboss.

Then Costello's problems dramatically increased. He was in and out of prison on contempt charges before the Kefauver Committee. Costello also faced denaturalization hearings, and he was convicted on some tax charges. Costello had become famous and all his political and police friends began hiding under their beds for fear of being linked with the notorious Mafioso.

CARLO GAMBINO

Gambino was the quiet, ambitious Underboss to Albert Anastasia. Unlike Anastasia, who was allied with Costello, Gambino was tight with Vito Genovese. We can assume that the two plotted to kill Costello. That failed, but Costello was out of power. Next, the two turned their sights on Albert Anastasia. As we discussed earlier, Anastasia had lost respect for not asking the Commission for permission to kill Boss Vincent Mangano and, if Bonanno is right, trying to kill Costello without a Commission vote.

Anastasia was vulnerable. As Jerry Capeci wrote in his column, Ganglandnews.com, it was not the Gallo brothers who killed Anastasia on October 25, 1957, but a crew under Gambino.

Gambino was going to be the new Boss, but there were others who wanted the throne. Bonanno certainly didn't want Gambino to be Boss. For Bonanno, the smart move was for him to support a friendly Gambino Capo for the throne. This way the man would be beholding to Bonanno and much more likely to form an alliance with him. Bonanno didn't want any rush to approve Gambino as Boss.

CONCLUSION:

Gambino, Genovese, and their staunch ally, Tommy Lucchese, wanted quick approval of the new state of affairs. Usually, the Commission would approve a new Boss, but this was an unusual situation. If the Commission approved Gambino and Genovese, both supported by Lucchese, it would appear that the Commission was endorsing itself. What was needed was the blessing of all the LCN Bosses and to do that, an out of sequence, National Meeting was called for Apalachin. This was the reason behind Apalachin.

PREPARATIONS:

On November 5, 1957, host Joe Barbara placed a $431.81 meat order, by phone, from Binghamton's Armour Company. The order was for twenty, ten-pound boxes of special cut steak for a total of two hundred pounds. There were two ten pound boxes of veal cutlets, one broiled ham, and one can of sliced luncheon meat. The meat was to be picked up on November 13.

DISCOVERED

Veteran NY State Trooper Sgt. Edgar Croswell had been suspicious of Joseph Barbara for some time. Those feelings were increased in October of 1956 when an aggressive Carmine Galante was stopped for speeding in the area. That led to the discovery of a connection between Galante and Barbara, plus the recent presence of other known hoods in nearby motels. By the time November 13, 1957, rolled around, Croswell was on the alert for any suspicious activities involving Barbara. The presence of two out of state vehicles at a local motel ignited his curiosity.

The next morning, Croswell, Trooper Vasisko, and two Bureau of Alcohol and Tax Agents, Ken Brown and Arthur Ruston, drove up to the Barbara estate. Vasisko was driving an unmarked NY State Trooper vehicle, and he pulled it into Barbara's driveway. The officers, never leaving their car, started jotting down license plate numbers. Suddenly, some men appeared from behind the garage and saw Croswell and his friends. All hell broke loose.

Vasisko drove the car down to the foot of the hill and parked it there. This was the only way out by vehicle. The officers decided that they would identify anyone who was leaving. At the same time, they were able to look up the hill, and they observed about a dozen men running towards the nearby woods. At this point, Croswell called for reinforcements.

WHO CAME TO LUNCH?

Below is a list of the Bosses, Acting Bosses, Underbosses, and Consiglieri who were identified as being at Barbara's. There were other men of lower rank as well. The Family names circa 1964 are used to avoid confusion.

Bonanno: Boss Joe Bonanno, former Underboss John Bonventre
Bufalino: Boss Joe Barbara, Underboss Russell Bufalino
Buffalo: Underboss John Montana
Cleveland: Boss John Scalish, Consigliere John DeMarco
Colombo: Boss Joe Profaci, Underboss Joe Magliocco
Dallas: Boss Joe Civello
Decavalcante (NJ): Underboss Louis Larasso
Denver: Boss James Colletti
Gambino: Boss Carlo Gambino
Genovese: Boss Vito Genovese, Underboss Gerry Catena, Consigliere Mike Miranda
Kansas City: Boss Nick Civella
Los Angeles: Boss Frank Desimone, Underboss Simone Scozzari
New England: Consigliere Frank Cucchiara
Philadelphia: Boss Joe Ida
Pittsburgh: Underboss Mike Genovese
Springfield: Boss Frank Zito
Tampa: Boss Santos Trafficante

WHO WAS MISSING?

Presumably, the Bosses of every La Cosa Nostra Family would have been invited to this National Meeting. Some were missing. Who were they?

CHICAGO

Boss Sam Giancanna was not identified at Apalachin. However, an illegal bug caught him talking about the affair. He boasted that if the event was held in Chicago, he had such control of the police that they would never have been bothered. Was Giancanna at Apalachin? The best guess is that he was running late and missed the show. It is hard to see the Chicago Outfit not having at least one representative there.

DETROIT

Boss Joe Zerilli was there but not detained. Evidence exists, in the form of his driver's license number, that he rented a car in nearby Binghamton. The Hertz clerk said the man looked wet and bedazzled.

NEW ORLEANS

On November 14, 1957, at 08:00 PM, Paul Scarcelli, 1140 Jackson Ave, New Orleans rented a car from Hertz in Endicott. The vehicle was returned to the same outlet three days later with 1,238 miles added to the odometer. The clerk claimed Scarcelli looked wet and bedazzled when he rented the vehicle.

From this information, gathered by a New York State Trooper, it is reasonable to speculate that someone higher in the New Orleans food chain was at Barbara's estate. Unfortunately, that name or names will probably never be known.

PITTSBURGH

Evidence exists that Boss John LaRocca was in the area, but he was not detected.

SAN JOSE

Boss Joe Cerrito was in the area. He was registered at the Hotel New Yorker, in the Big Apple, on November 11 through November 14. But on November 13, Cerrito had moved over to the Hotel Casey in Scranton, New York, not too far from Barbara's. He either made an undetected escape from the estate or was merely late getting there. Since Russell Bufalino was with Cerrito at the Hotel Casey and Cerrito had no car, it's reasonable to assume Bufalino took Cerrito to Barbara's.

SAN FRANCISCO

Underboss James Lanza was close by as well. He was with Joe Cerrito in New York and at the Hotel Casey in Scranton, NY, on November 13.

Like Cerrito, it is reasonable to assume Lanza was taken to Barbara's but escaped undetected.

ST. LOUIS

Boss Anthony Lopiparo and Underboss Anthony Giordano were most likely not in attendance nor in the area. In September of 1956, both men were convicted of a tax conspiracy and sentenced to four years. They were out on bond until they lost their appeals and went to prison in 1958. It's likely they both had restrictions on their bond release and didn't want to take the chance of going to Apalachin.

CONCLUSION:

The 1957 fiasco at Apalachin was one of the worst days for La Cosa Nostra. Now, no one, including FBI Director J. Edgar Hoover, and a host of politicians, could deny the existence of organized crime in the form of La Cosa Nostra. Twenty-nine years later, this evidence would be used in the Commission case. The hurts just kept on coming.

CHAPTER FOURTEEN

Major Decisions: Part One

From 1931 onward, the Commission was faced with many life-changing decisions. For example, the fiasco at Apalachin has been discussed earlier. In this space, it is impossible to examine all major events that involved the Commission, but we have selected four to give the reader some idea of what problems the Commission faced and how they dealt with them.

THE GALLO WAR: Part One

When specific events from the Gallo war would make the newspapers, most observers thought that this was just a gang of regular guys battling against the big, underworld powers. In a sense this was true, but the real story is much more complicated than that.

THE GALLOS

There were three Gallo boys; Larry, the oldest, Joey, the wildest, and Albert, the youngest and most inexperienced. They had all grown up in the rough neighborhood of Red Hook, which was in Brooklyn right up against the East River. Like so many other hoods mentioned in this book, the Gallos grew up tough and took few prisoners.

Money and power were at the root of their discontent. They were always scrounging around trying to make a good score. The more successful hoods were either involved in long-standing gambling rackets or had their hooks into some union local that not only provide a regular salary but plenty of opportunities to extort money. The Gallos were small timers and resented it.

SHOWTIME

Larry and Joey Gallo got a big boost to their egos and reputations when they appeared before the Senate Rackets Committee, in 1959. At the time, the Gallos were involved in the jukebox rackets, which basically meant they were extorting anyone connected to jukeboxes. To hide their extortion/coercion, they created a union local so the payments could be attributed to "initiation fees," "dues," and other labels.

During their Senate appearance, the Gallos, like all other hoods, took the Fifth. However, it was Joey's appearance and manner that made everyone take notice. For one thing, he wore sunglasses, which added to an aura of menace.

Probably due to the sensation that the Gallo's appearance caused, it wasn't long before a Nassau grand jury was handing down indictments against the Gallos and John O'Rouke, a Teamster Union power and many others. Joey Gallo was convicted of coercion and given a year in the slammer. He did three months before being released.

FRANK "FRANKIE SHOTS" ABBATEMARCO

The next big event for the Gallos was the November 4, 1959 murder of numbers (gambling) kingpin Frank "Frankie Shots" Abbatemarco. The Gallos had been associated with Abbatemarco for an extended period of time. Back in 1952, Abbatemarco had been charged with running a $2,500,000 numbers operation. Joey and Larry got swept up in the arrests.

Abbatemarco had been a high ranking member of Joe Profaci's (Colombo) Family for years but somehow had gotten into Profaci's bad books. A dispute over money would be the most reasonable guess. The hit order went down the chain of authority, ending up on the desk of Larry Gallo. Abbatemarco was dead.

It is logical to think that the Gallos would believe they would be rewarded by being given at least a piece of Abbatemarco's numbers operation. Apparently, that didn't happen, according to most accounts of the Gallos early days. However, primary source evidence on that long-accepted theory is hard to come by. It is not entirely sure that this was at the root of the coming revolt by the Gallos.

JOE PROFACI

Profaci had ruled his Family, since the late 1920s, with little turmoil. However, the late 1950s and early 1960s were not kind to him. Below is a brief summary of some of his troubles. They are essential for they distracted and weakened him, thus making him appear vulnerable to the Mafia predators lurking in the weeds.

November 14/57
Profaci was identified as being at Apalachin. This caused massive amounts of unwanted publicity.

December 9/57
Profaci was ordered deported.

December 16/57
FBI Director J. Edgar Hoover gave permission for his agents to begin secretly opening Profaci's mail. This would last for 30 days.

March 24/28
Profaci submitted to an FBI interview

October 31/58
Profaci entered the hospital. He remained for a few days, complaining of headaches, etc. (these were signs of his future brain tumor)

January 13/59
Profaci testified before the New York State Commission of Investigations. He only made a few, brief family-related answers, before begging off sick.

January 27/59
Before the NY State Commission of Investigations, Profaci's lawyer explained that his client was ill. Eventually, Profaci was given immunity, and he then answered questions about Apalachin.

January 12/60
Profaci won his denaturalization appeal. (He wouldn't be deported)

January 13/60
Profaci was sentenced to 5 years and fined $10,000, for conspiracy to obstruct justice, by refusing to give reasons for the Apalachin meeting. (Some other Mafia leaders were also convicted. Eventually, an appeals court overturned all the convictions)

March 22/60
A Marshall's sale auctioned off some of Profaci's properties to meet a tax lien.

THE CONSPIRACY

By February of 1961, the Gallos were still broke and frustrated. Profaci was jammed up with endless legal problems. His fragile health began a rapid decline. Carlo Gambino, Boss of the Gambino Family, and his close ally, Tommy Lucchese, Boss of the Lucchese Family, saw a golden opportunity.

Gambino and Lucchese wanted to control the Commission. To do so, they first needed to have Profaci removed. The second step would be to manage who was elected the new Boss. In 1961, they believed that their best strategy would be to play with the discontent of the Gallos and encourage them to revolt. So far so good.

PEACE ATTEMPTS

FBI informer Greg Scarpa gave his handlers some background on the Gallo revolt. He related that there were a series of sit-downs at the Golden Door Restaurant at Idlewild Airport (today's JFK). Scarpa said he only attended two meetings for he couldn't stand Joey Gallo's conduct. It can be reasonably assumed there were many other sit-downs over the Gallo's grievances.

ALLIANCES

The Gallos didn't start their revolt alone. Here's what their close associate Pete "The Greek" Diapoulos said, "At first everyone wanted it: Junior Persico's crew, the Renaldi and Bat brothers, Vinny the Sidge, Abby, and a lot of other guys." Greg Scarpa told his FBI handlers that Carmine "Junior" Persico had tried to convince him to join with the Gallos. (Scarpa declined).

As noted above, the Gallos were getting semi-secret support from Carlo Gambino and Tommy Lucchese, who had their own agenda. Also backing the Gallos, was Capo Tony Bender of the Genovese Family. He had some leeway to manoeuver, since his Boss, Vito Genovese, was in prison.

THE KIDNAPPINGS

In early February 1961, the Gallos made their big move. They kidnapped four or five Profaci (Colombo) men and just missed their primary target, Profaci himself. It was a stunning, daring, and dangerous move. It would seem logical that it wouldn't have happened unless the Gallos felt their backs were covered by a Commission power. Bonanno wrote, "To bolster their position... the Gallos sought the support of another Family head, Carlo Gambino."

THE VICTIMS

All sources agree that Underboss Joe Magliocco and Capo Frank Profaci were victims. Then things get confusing. Peter "Pete the Greek" Diapoulos, a close associate of the Gallos, claims the other two men were John Scimone, and future Boss Joe Colombo. But back on March 2, 1962, Gambino Capo Mike Clemente was secretly taped, saying the men were; Underboss Magliocco, Capo Frank Profaci, Capo Sal Mussachio, and Capo Harry Fontana. Whoever the four victims were, the glaring absence of Boss Joe Profaci considerably weakened the Gallo's position.

NEGOTIATIONS

On February 23, 1961, Consigliere Charles "Charlie the Sidge" Locicero and another senior Profaci (Colombo) member, visited the Gallos at their President Street HQ. Thanks to Inspector Ray Martin, of the NYPD, and his informers, we have a good understanding of what was discussed. First of all, Locicero was smart enough to let the Gallos vent a little.

In summary, their main complaint was the killing of Frank "Frankie Shots" Abbatemarco, back in 1959. The Gallos had been ordered to do the hit, and they carried it out efficiently. Later they learned the reason for the murder was that Abbatemarco was behind in his tribute payments to Profaci.

For the Gallos, that was unacceptable. They believed "Frankie Shots" should have been given time to catch up. Probably of more importance was the fact Abbatemarco's gambling operation went to the Underboss, rather than the Gallos. There were other grievances, but the main one was about the Abbatemarco situation. The Gallos were broke and wanted money. According to Inspector Martin, their price for peace was $150,000 ($2,250,000 in today's dollars)

Locicero was a good listener. When the Gallos were done, he quietly asked about the fate of the hostages. He was given assurances that they would be safe, while negotiations continued.

Gallo associate Peter Diapoulos had a somewhat different version of that sit-down. He related that Profaci had sent word that, "He wouldn't negotiate until his men were released unharmed."

Diapoulos went on to explain that Joey Gallo wanted to kill one hostage to show Profaci they meant business. Brother Larry strongly disagreed, and a fight nearly broke out. Joey and his wife then took off to California to cool off for a few weeks.

FBI reports indicated that the Gallos then conferred with powerful Genovese Capo Tony Bender on February 26, 1961. While it is unclear what was discussed, following events certainly give us an indication.

On February 28, 1961, the hostages were released and a calm settled over Brooklyn. However, everyone was holding their breaths, for this undoubtedly was just the beginning of something.

WARFARE

For the next seven months, the Gallos were living in a real-life shooting gallery as this summary of events demonstrates.

May 11/61
Joey Gallo and three others were arrested for the attempted extortion of businessman Teddy Moss. This case would come back to hogtie Gallo.

June 12/61
Profaci forces fired shots at Punchy Illiano, a veteran Gallo crew member

June 19/61
Alfred Mondella was gunned down. It was believed he was supplying guns to the Gallos.

July 25/61
A shot was fired at Frank Lettiere, who was driving Larry Gallo's vehicle.

August 1961
Carmine Persico and Jiggs Forlano deserted the Gallos and returned to the Profaci fold.

August 16/61
Violent Gallo mobster Joe Gioelli disappeared. He was a significant loss to the Gallos.

ATTEMPTED KILLING OF LARRY GALLO

For some reason, Larry Gallo agreed to meet Profaci (Colombo) Soldier John Scimone, at the Sahara Lounge, at the corner of Utica and Clarendon, in Brooklyn. Pete Diapoulos later wrote that Albert Gallo argued with Larry that he was being suckered, but Larry went anyway. It was a mistake.

On Aug 20, 1961, around 5 PM, Larry Gallo entered the Sahara Lounge with Scimone. The place was empty, except for bartender Charley Clemenza, because opening time was 6 PM. Gallo and Scimone stood at the bar having a few drinks when suddenly a rope was wrapped around Gallo's neck and pulled tight.

Gallo eventually fell to the floor unconscious but won the lottery. Just then Sergeant Meagher of the NYPD stepped into the bar. Meagher was curious because he knew the place was not to open till 6 PM. The police officer saw Gallo's legs and immediately three men raced from the saloon.

In the melee, patrolman Melvin Blei was wounded in the face. The three hoods tore off in a white Caddy. It was found four blocks away with a banged up John Scimone lying in the gutter. The others had disappeared, most likely picked up by a backup car.

Surprisingly, Larry Gallo signed a complaint, which acknowledged that the cops figured two of the hitmen were Carmine Persico and Sally D'Ambrosio. The FBI later discovered, through an informant, that the man in charge of the hit team was Capo Mimi Scialo, a Profaci loyalist.

THE HITS JUST KEEP ON COMING

August 22/61
NYPD raided the Gallo HQ on President Street and arrested 11 of the Gallo crew. Apparently, this was an attempt to head off Gallo retaliation attacks.

August 24/61.
"Big Lollipop Carna, a Gallo, was wounded near the Gallo HQ.

October 4/61
A carload of Gallo hoods went out hunting for Profaci targets. They saw Capo Harry Fontana on a sidewalk and stopped. Suddenly hothead Joe Magnasco jumped out of the vehicle and started berating Fontana. That argument came to a quick end when Fontana's brother pulled out a pistol and unloaded it into Magnasco, who promptly fell dead in the street while everyone else bailed.

October 5/61
Carmine Persico and John Scimone were indicted for the attempted murder of Larry Gallo.

October 10/61
NYPD raided the Gallo HQ for the second time. 13 Gallos were arrested, and their pictures made the papers.

October 21/61
Joey Gallo was on trial for the attempted extortion of Teddy Moss on May 11, 1961.

November 11/61
John Guariglio and Paul Rico were killed. Decades later, it is alleged the hits were done on orders from Joey Gallo.

November 15/61
Yet another raid on Gallo HQ was conducted.

December 2/61
Someone tried to kill Larry Gallo with a shotgun but missed.

ANOTHER PEACE ATTEMPT

On December 5, 1961, FBI informant Greg Scarpa told his handlers, that orders had come down from the Boss to stop all hostilities. A few weeks later, Joey Gallo was convicted of the extortion of Teddy Moss and was sentenced to 7 years 3 months to 14 years 6 months. At the end of December, Consigliere Charles Locicero made another peace bid with the Gallos, but they rejected his compromises on January 9, 1962.

According to Joe Bonanno, it is at this time that Boss Carlo Gambino called for a meeting of the Commission. It turned out that Gambino had met with the Gallos and heard their grievances and agreed to present them to the Commission.

As Bonanno tells it, Gambino acted like a kind advisor, lamenting the problems in the Profaci (Colombo) Family and suggesting it was time for Profaci to retire, relax and leave the troubles for a new Boss to settle. Boss Tommy Lucchese echoed Gambino's sentiments. It was clear these two were secretly working with the Gallos to unseat Profaci. Bonanno wrote that he strongly supported Profaci, so no vote was taken on his future. It was status quo, but it was clear Profaci was in trouble.

On March 18, 1962, Larry Gallo visited Consigliere Locicero and told him that the moratorium would end at 6 PM the next day. Later, Scarpa told the FBI that the moratorium on violence would continue to April 2, 1962. He also added that Locicero was working to convince Profaci to step down. That didn't happen.

Profaci was infuriated with the Gallos and his rivals on the Commission. He sent an ultimatum to the Gallos, who had three choices; they could stay out of the organization and be peaceful, the Gallos could come back into the organization with guarantees, but the offer didn't apply to their men, and finally, if the Gallos continued their rebellion, then Profaci would retaliate against them AND their wives.

Profaci's long-standing ill health finally caught up to him. He passed away on June 6, 1962.

CONCLUSION

The Commission was an ineffective body during this part of the Gallo War. One member was under siege (Profaci) while two (Gambino and Lucchese) were quietly plotting against Profaci. Joe Bonanno was struggling to support Profaci, but was beginning to feel isolated and not supported by his cousin, fellow Commission member Stefano Magaddino of Buffalo. It was a mess.

CHAPTER FIFTEEN

Major Decisions: Part Two

Boss Joe Bonanno, trying to control the Commission, set off the most significant crisis that body had to face up until the Commission Indictment in 1985. The major events of this conflict are outlined below.

THE BANANA WAR

As described in previous chapters, Joe Bonanno was a proud and ambitious Sicilian, who rose through the ranks of La Cosa Nostra during the violent years of the late 1920s and early 1930s. In 1931, Bonanno had been elected Boss of his own Family, plus he became an original Commission member.

WARNING SHOTS

When Boss Albert Anastasia was killed, in October of 1957, Bonanno was on vacation in Italy. It seems most likely that Bonanno was on the losing side when the Commission decided whether to kill Anastasia or not. To distance himself from the publicity the killing of Anastasia would inevitably bring, Bonanno booked a trip to Italy.

Upon his return, Bonanno claimed to be astonished that a National Meeting had been called for November 14, 1957, in Apalachin, New York.

In his autobiography, Bonanno made some brazen lies. He stated that he was both opposed to the gathering and furthermore, Bonanno denied he was ever present. His claims were ridiculous and easily disproven.

For example, he made up a story that the reason he was identified as being at Apalachin was that a friend was carrying his driver's license, which had just been renewed. The man forgot to give it to Bonanno in New York and therefore had it on him when he was detained and identified at Apalachin.

The problem was that Bonanno had been identified, not only by his driver's license but also by his Social Security card. Furthermore, his relative and former Underboss, John Bonventre, who was also detained at Apalachin, told the NY State Troopers that he had come to Apalachin with Bonanno. Case closed.

THE GALLO WAR: Part Two

As we have seen in the previous chapter, Bonanno made a desperate move to support his beleaguered friend Joe Profaci. (Colombo Family) Fellow Commission members Carlo Gambino and Tommy Lucchese were trying to unseat Profaci but were thwarted by Bonanno's counter move. They were not happy nor was Bonanno.

THE CONSPIRACY

In 1962, Joe Profaci had died of natural causes, and the throne was open. Gambino and Lucchese desperately wanted to place a friendly face on the top slot and automatically on the Commission. That meant they had to prevent the elevation of Profaci (Colombo) Underboss Joe Magliocco. Bonanno needed just the opposite. The stage was set for a major war.

The keys to Bonanno's frustrations were Carlo Gambino and Tommy Lucchese. Bonanno decided the best way to take care of that problem was to whack out both of them and have people sympathetic to him placed on the thrones of their families. Bonanno was not stupid enough to attempt this move himself. He knew his cousin Stefano Magaddino, Boss of Buffalo, was no longer a supporter and perhaps even a deadly rival. The only person Bonanno could turn to was the beleaguered Joe Magliocco, Underboss to the late Joe Profaci.

The first step was to get Magliocco on the Colombo Family throne by having a vote of the Capos. They would also vote for Consigliere, and the nominee was Salvatore Mussachia. The first group voted on June 28, 1962.

Three days later the rest of the Capos voted, including Greg Scarpa, an FBI informant. Not surprisingly, Magliocco was elected the new Boss and Mussachia the Consigliere. Ambrose Magliocco, the Boss' brother, told Scarpa that this vote would be presented to the Commission for approval.

Fifteen days later, the word was being passed around that Magliocco had appointed Joe Colombo, Sonny Franzese, and Tom DiBella as Capos. Former Consigliere Charles LoCicero was out in the cold and not happy.

THE KEY TO STABILITY

Magliocco knew that the only way he was going to be safe on the throne was to wipe out the Gallo revolt. This would also undercut the machinations of Carlo Gambino and Tommy Lucchese who wanted Magliocco out and their own man in as his replacement.

On August 7/62 Scarpa told his FBI handlers that Boss Magliocco had informed him that every member of the Family would be assessed $100 a week to compensate the crews who were hunting Gallos.

Meanwhile, former Consigliere Charles Locicero was doing everything he could to undermine Magliocco. At one point, he told Scarpa to whack out Magliocco, but that never happened. In fact, the FBI warned Scarpa that under no circumstances was he to participate in a murder.

In October 1962, Joey Gallo went off to prison to serve his extortion sentence. Despite his absence, the Gallos kept fighting. In January 1963, they planted a bomb under Carmine Persico's car. It was Persico who was leading the charge against the Gallos. The bomb went "BOOM" but Persico, shaken but not dead, stumbled out of his vehicle. Everyone was stunned. Four months later, the Gallos ambushed Persico in his car. Although he was gravely wounded, Persico survived again. The Gallos had pathetic luck.

Behind the scenes, maneuvering was continually going on. Some Capos, secretly backed by Gambino and Lucchese, urged Magliocco to step down. Joe Bonanno was furious because things were not going his way at all.

In July, the Persico crew gunned down close Gallo associate, Hassan Ali Waffa. The next month, the Gallos killed Joseph "Bats" Cardiello in the morning of August 9, 1963. That afternoon the Magliocco forces retaliated and murdered Gallo member Louis Mariani and wounded Anthony Getch.

DOWNFALL

Seeing that Magliocco's plan to wipe out the Gallos was going south, Joe Bonanno hatched a plot with Magliocco to strike at the real leaders of the rebellion, Carlo Gambino, and Tommy Lucchese. Magliocco made plans and finally gave the order for the hits to go down. It was a disaster.

In his autobiography, Joe Bonanno concocted a ridiculous story to explain how he got tangled up in this mess. He claimed his son ended up living at Magliocco's home because of a marital dispute. According to Bonanno, his son had no choice but to accept the offer of hospitality from the beleaguered Magliocco. Any reasonable father, knowing the dangerous situation, would have insisted his son stay at a hotel rather than in the middle of the fire. The real story was that Bonanno's son was at Magliocco's to show his enemies that Joe Bonanno was supporting him.

Then Bonanno tried to explain away the fact that his son Bill drove to a train station with Magliocco, where the Boss passed on the order to start the attack on Gambino and Lucchese. Both Joe and Bill, in his own autobiography, claimed that Bill had no idea what was going on. No one believed them then, and no one believes them now.

According to Bonanno, "Colombo (a Magliocco Capo) apparently decided that he would have more to gain if he betrayed Magliocco and switched sides." Colombo ran to Gambino, and it was all over for Magliocco. He was hauled before the Gambino dominated Commission and put on trial. A hidden FBI bug in the office of Commission member Stefano Magaddino, heard him relate what Magliocco said, "Yes, I condemned them (Gambino and Lucchese) to death." Magliocco was fined $43,000 and ordered to step down as Boss and to call for new elections. Magliocco escaped with his life only to die of a heart attack in December of 1963.

BONANNO ON THE HOTSEAT

On September 13, 1963, an illegal FBI bug overheard New England Boss Ray Patriarca tell Gallo crew member Nicky Bianco, that the Commission had approved his induction. This needs some explaining.

Bianca was a Patriarca Associate who had moved to New York and hooked up with the Gallo gang. In September 1963, it appeared that the Gallo War would finally be coming to an end. This would require some peace meetings (sit-downs) between the Gallos and the new leader of the Colombo Family. Unfortunately for the Gallos, their only official members of the Mafia, Larry, and Joey were locked up. It had to be a "made" man to represent them hence the decision for Bianco to approach Patriarca for help. On September 25, 1963, Bianco got his button which is another way of saying he was formally inducted into La Cosa Nostra.

RSVP

Gambino and Lucchese knew they had Bonanno by the neck. They could prove he was plotting their deaths and now wanted to expel him from the Commission. But they tried to pretend they were just conducting a non-biased investigation. Bonanno had too much experience to fall for that ploy. He started bouncing all over the country so he could claim he had not received the RSVP.

O CANADA 1

On April 4, 1964, a meeting of the Bonanno Capos resulted in them rubber-stamping Bill Bonanno's elevation to Consigliere. (Bill was a son of Joe Bonanno) Decades later, Bonanno tried to demonstrate that the Capos were acting on their own free will. Bonanno claimed to have been in Canada when the Consigliere election took place. Readers of his book might have been deceived in by this statement, but an examination of the facts show that Bonanno didn't enter Canada till May 25, 1964. There was no way Bonanno wasn't directly involved in having his son elected Consigliere.

Bonanno thought this was a smart move, but it tore his Family apart. His long-time friend Gaspar DiGregorio, a Capo in the Family, felt he was entitled to the Consigliere position due to his loyal service over many decades. Devastated at the snub, DiGregorio immediately complained to his friend Stefano Magaddino, Boss of the Buffalo Family who was a power on the Commission.

Magaddino urged DiGregorio to boycott Bonanno Family meetings. He did that, and as a consequence, DiGregorio was "put on the shelf" (frozen out) by Bonanno. The crisis was now escalating out of control.

In May, Bonanno traveled to Montreal, Canada. The Bonanno Family had a branch plant there since the mid-fifties. Evidence exists that he met with Joseph Saputo, the owner of a small cheese making plant. Paperwork indicates that Saputo and Bonanno agreed that Bonanno would invest in the company in return for twenty percent of the business. So far so good for Bonanno.

Bonanno then applied for permission to immigrate to Canada legally. Bonanno later claimed he was never intending to obtain Canadian citizenship. The paperwork contradicts this brazen lie. In any case, the RCMP (Royal

Canadian Mounted Police) got involved and arrested Bonanno and held him for possible deportation. This became significant news in both Canada and the United States. The suspicious Commission was now sure Bonanno was going to set up an independent Family, in Montreal. We know this from an FBI bug in Buffalo Boss Stefano Magaddino's office.

On July 30, 1964, Bonanno was deported to Chicago where a subpoena from a grand jury awaited him. Bonanno was now under pressure from both his enemies on the Commission and the government as well.

DEPOSED:

Early in September 1964, the Commission met to discuss the Bonanno problem yet again. The result was that Bonanno was formally expelled from La Cosa Nostra. He was replaced by long-time Capo Gaspar DiGregorio. As the month progressed, illegal FBI bugs picked up the spreading of the expulsion order to other LCN Bosses. A brief summary of a few of those messages follows.

September 29/64
Frank DeSimone, Boss of the Los Angeles Family, traveled to San Francisco to tell that city's Boss that Bonanno was out.

September 30/64
Tommy Eboli, Acting Boss of the Genovese Family and his Underboss, Gerry Catena, traveled to the Providence Rhode Island headquarters of Raymond Patriarca, Boss of the New England Family. They explained that Bonanno had been dethroned.

September 31/64
Gerry Catena, the Underboss of the Genovese Family, was taped ordering his crew to have nothing to do with Bonanno Family members till a new Boss was selected.

It is clear that Bonanno was dumped by the Commission. Not surprisingly, Bonanno began to question the legitimacy of that body. Theoretically, the membership of the Commission was supposed to be ratified every five years after its formation in 1931. That took place up until 1956. The subsequent ratification was scheduled for 1961, but the 1957 fiasco at Apalachin ended any thoughts of holding another National Meeting any time soon. Consequently, in 1961, the sitting Commission members ratified themselves for another five years. In 1964, Bonanno suddenly began claiming the Commission was illegitimate and thus couldn't dethrone him. Everyone ignored him.

KIDNAPPING

Bonanno's long run of terrible tactical and strategic moves came to a head just after midnight on October 21, 1964. In front of witnesses, he was "kidnapped" in the street and rushed away in a vehicle. It was an incredible event and made headlines all over North America. What had happened?

BONANNO'S VERSION

In his 1983 autobiography, Bonanno claimed he had been kidnapped by Stefano Magaddino's men and held captive for six weeks in an isolated farmhouse, presumably somewhere near Buffalo. He went on to state that Magaddino would frequently appear and the two men would discuss and argue their different opinions on the Bonanno crisis and even some philosophical theories. Bonanno's description of Magaddino was nearly entirely negative.

THE REAL STORY

Bonanno had himself kidnapped to avoid appearing in court. There he would have had to take the Fifth Amendment and would have ended up in prison on contempt charges just like his son and many other closed mouthed Mafiosi. Bonanno would have been entirely incapable of forging a "come back" if he was locked up. Of lesser importance was his plan to keep his rivals off balance, for they would not know where he was.

The Proof:

October 21/64
Bonanno said he was forced into a car and had to sit between two men on the long ride to the farmhouse. (We presume a third man was driving the vehicle for this was long before self-driving cars.)

Bill Bonanno wrote that there were only two kidnappers. One drove, and the other sat beside Bonanno in the back.

October 21/64
New Jersey Boss Sam Decavalcante's conversation with a subordinate left the distinct impression he had no idea what was happening. (A Bonanno supporter might challenge this by claiming that Sam the Plumber wasn't in on the Commission's kidnap plotting.)

October 22/64
Decavalcante told his men that he had been with Gerry Catena, the Genovese Family Underboss. Sam said Catena had no idea what was going on. Sam's Underboss speculated that Bonanno kidnapped himself to avoid a subpoena. The same day FBI agents interviewed Commission member Angelo Bruno. He said he believed Bonanno kidnapped himself.

November 23/64.
Decavalcante told some of his men that he had met with Carlo Gambino and Tommy Lucchese, both Commission members, and Tampa Boss Santos Trafficante. They all believed Bonanno kidnapped himself.

December 2/64
Bonanno claimed he was released a month and a half after the kidnapping. That would put his release on or about this date. Bonanno's version of how he traveled to Tucson varies somewhat from that of his son Bill.

Bonanno then claimed he waited two weeks before having someone call his son Bill, to tell him he was safe. This strains all credulity. Not letting his family know he was safe, would have been great cruelty. He was lying, as usual. See below.

December 9/64
Bonanno loyalist Capo Joe Notaro was taped telling Boss Sam "The Plumber" Decavalcante that there was a recent meeting of the Bonanno Capos. Both Bonanno and his son were present. So much for Bonanno's claim that he didn't contact his son for two weeks.

December 17/64

Bill Bonanno claimed that this is the day he received a mysterious phone call telling him, for the first time, that his father was safe. This was a total lie as the entry above shows.

THE TROUTMAN STREET AMBUSH: NOT!

On January 28, 1966, young Bill Bonanno showed that his thinking was just as crazy as his father's, regarding how to handle the crisis. Bill, along with some Associates, staged a shootout on Troutman Street, in Brooklyn. They ran around firing off shots then headed for the hills. Bill was trying to make it appear that the Bonanno opponents were acting recklessly and creating a public relations nightmare for the Mafia. The thinking was that the Commission might withdraw their support for the insurgents. Oops!

No one paid any attention to the supposed Friday night shootout/ambush. Bill Bonanno was very frustrated. On Monday, he called a gullible reporter on the New York Times and told him about the wild gunfight. The reporter repeated the story to the Time's Metropolitan Editor.

The next day, Tuesday, February 1, 1964, there was a little story about the shooting. Because it is in the Times the story was picked up by other media outlets. Suddenly, a fake shootout became "fact," and it has remained "fact" to the present day because it has been repeated over and over again in books, TV shows and the like.

Perhaps the most pathetic account of this fake event was provided by Bill Bonanno in his book, "Bound by Honor," published in 1999. Bill Bonanno detailed a heroic, Rambo style, escape from certain death as they left a residence where a peace meeting was to have taken place. His accomplices were all conveniently dead when he made these ludicrous claims.

Bill said they were under machine gun, pistol, and shotgun fire. (No one reported any shooting that night). He stated that he and his confederates unloaded a hailstorm of bullets into a vehicle containing two men. (This was never reported by anyone). Son Bill could undoubtedly tell an exciting story. It wasn't true.

Way back in 1971, in Gaye Talese's, "Man of Honor," Bill Bonanno related a much more sedate version of the ambush. In this account, Bill and his boys were not leaving the house, but they were approaching the residence when the trap happened. He described being fired upon, from many locations (remember—no one reported any shots that night). Bill went on to explain how he escaped. There was NO mention of shooting up the car when Bonanno and his men ran around the corner.

The truth of the matter is that Bill Bonanno lied about the incident when he recounted it to Gaye Talese in the 1960's and embellished his fable in 1999. The trouble was that Bill Bonanno was too lazy to check his past stories and make sure they were aligned. (Of course, this was true about nearly all his fanciful tales.)

THE RETURN

Joe Bonanno's disappearance had brought down tons of heat on all the Mafia Families. There were many grand juries, hundreds of subpoenas went out, some hoods were locked up for not co-operating, and the police and feds were continually harassing the gangsters. It was nearly impossible for them to conduct their rackets. Something had to give.

On May 17, 1966, Joe Bonanno surrendered to authorities in New York. The constant police pressure on his personal family and men had taken its toll. Another critical factor was that the IRS was about to confiscate Bonanno property in Tucson. He was quickly released on bond and immediately continued plotting to regain his throne.

Frank Mari, a future Bonanno Family Underboss, was wounded by machine gun fire by the Bonanno followers on July 13, 1966. This gun will become important later.

O CANADA 2

By 1966, the Bonanno loyalists were broke. With all the defections the regular tribute money was no longer pouring in. The rackets of the loyalist had also dried up due to police pressure. Consigliere Bill Bonanno made a desperate move and headed north to Montreal, where a very successful Bonanno Family crew had been operating under Capo Vincent Cotroni.

From the bug in Sam the Plumber' office, the FBI learned that the Montreal crew did not want to get involved in the war. The new Bonanno administration and the Commission agreed to this. Now Bill Bonanno was attempting to change things. Thanks to informers and bugs the RCMP knew Bonanno was in Montreal and acted accordingly.

On November 28, 1966, Bill Bonanno and a group of his supporters were arrested in Montreal. Four were charged with illegal gun possession whereas Bonanno faced a driving without a license charge. They were all quickly deported. Oddly enough, in his autobiography, Bill Bonanno denied this event ever happened. It is unclear whether they got any money out of the very uncomfortable Cotroni.

Gaspar DiGregorio's reign at the top of the Bonanno Family was a short one. Ill health and the lack of ambition and aggression made him ineffective. On Oct 31, 1967, the FBI learned that the Commission had approved veteran Capo Paul Sciacca as the new Boss.

CYPRESS GARDENS MASSACRE

Three anti-Bonanno men were machine-gunned to death on November 10, 1967, in a Queen's restaurant called the Cypress Gardens. The prime target was Thomas D'Angelo, a Bonanno Capo who was allied with new Boss Paul Sciacca. A brother and an associate went down in the firestorm. It was an outrageous action that put many innocent lives in danger yet Bill Bonanno, believing his readers are idiots, claimed, "The shooting was surgically precise."

If that was the case, the bullets which went through the front window and into the street must have been planned as well. Bonanno deliberately lied as he tried to justify this outrageous event. He inserted a second gunman and claims the plan was for the machine gunner to shoot over everyone's heads to distract their attention, while the second hitman killed the primary victim and the other two men. This was the same machine gun that wounded Frank Mari on July 13/66.

Like most of Bonanno's stories, this is nonsense. There wasn't a second shooter. Ballistics showed that all the bullets came from the same machine gun. The many witnesses related that there was a lone gunner. That the Bonannos would stoop to such a low level to kill a rival surely makes a mockery of their claim to be men of "Honor."

GOOD RIDDANCE

Joe Bonanno suffered his third heart attack in February of 1968 and moved permanently to Tucson Arizona. At that point, the Fat Lady had sung and Bonanno's time at the top of a Mafia Family was over. Unfortunately, a few mutts were hard of hearing, so sporadic back and forth killings went on for a few more years. The Commission edict that Bonanno was out as Boss was finally fulfilled. No one felt sorry for the Bonannos.

CHAPTER SIXTEEN

Preparations

In 1981, the feds decided to get their act together and really go after La Cosa Nostra. No longer would they attack individuals and their crimes. They were now looking for a pattern of crimes committed by members of specific New York Mafia Families. In other words, they were finally going to use all the tools made available to them as provided in the 1968 Omnibus Crime Control and Safe Streets Act, and the 1970 Organized Crime Control Act. The latter contained the RICO statutes and the witness protection program. The former legally permitted court-approved electronic surveillance. La Cosa Nostra was going to be blasted with a tsunami that they would never forget.

Exhibit #36 from page 859 of "Organized Crime: 25 Years after Valachi" (Hearings before the Permanent Subcommittee on Investigations) outlines the strategy best. A copy of the exhibit is in the appendix of the report. A very simplified summary of the testimony of Supervisory Special Agent James Kossler follows.

The FBI had to collect evidence to show that "The Enterprise," in our discussion, the Mafia Family, existed. Secondly, they had to show that each targeted member of that Family had committed two criminal acts, within ten years of each other. These are called the "predicate acts." If these steps were proven, the individuals could be sentenced under the harsh penalties of RICO conspiracy (planning) and RICO (carrying out the crimes).

STRATEGY

The FBI reorganized their forces in New York City so that five units were dedicated to taking down one of the Genovese, Gambino, Colombo, Lucchese and Bonanno Families.

Eventually, another critical component was added. New York State formed some task forces that significantly contributed to the decimation of the Five Families. Ron Goldstock headed up one such unit, whose work significantly affected many cases, including the Commission trial.

After much infighting, FBI headquarters bought into the enterprise method of attacking LCN and provided adequate resources to make this possible. This was a process, not a onetime deal where everything was granted to the New York Office. These struggles are outlined in Jules Bonavolonta's excellent book, "The Good Guys: How We Turned the FBI 'Round—and Finally Broke the Mob."

THE BONANNO FAMILY

Undercover FBI agent Joe Pistone had bravely infiltrated the Bonanno Family in the late 1970s. His efforts are described in his successful book, "Donnie Brasco." On November 23, 1981, a number of his Bonanno Family Associates were indicted on RICO charges, including the murder of the three Bonanno Capos back on May 5, 1981. In the fall of 1982, Pistone's Mafia mentor, Benjamin "Lefty" Ruggiero and three other Bonanno Soldiers, were convicted on various charges.

Future Boss Joey Massino avoided trial by going on the run. Capo Dominick "Sonny Black" Napolitano was nowhere to be found either.

THE PIZZA CONNECTION

When Carmine Galante was whacked out in the summer of 1979, the investigation began to focus on a wing of the Bonanno Family which was referred to as the Sicilians or the Zips. This was because most of them either were recent immigrants from Sicily or they maintained close contacts with their homeland.

Eventually, the FBI latched on to a vast drug conspiracy mainly centered on Bonanno Capo, Sal Catalano. The investigation kept expanding and expanding ending up with an indictment of some 38 men. Below is an immensely simplified outline of what was happening.

New York Associates of Catalano were importing heroin from Sicily and moving money in the opposite direction. Meanwhile, a few of those Associates were also buying heroin from relatives of Gaetano Badalamente. The latter was once Boss of Bosses in Sicily, but he and his allies had been overpowered by a rival group.

Badalamente fled to South America but continued to sell heroin to make a living. Dealing with him was extremely dangerous, for it would provoke extreme violence from his enemies. The book, "Last Days of the Sicilians" by Ralph Blumenthal, does an excellent job of telling these very complicated stories.

In March 1987, most of the Pizza Connection defendants were found guilty of a variety of charges. Regarding the power structure of the Bonanno Family, the guilty verdict for Sal Catalano, and his following 45-year sentence removed him and his Sicilians from the higher levels of the Family. Not surprisingly, the heroin kept on coming.

JOEY MASSINO

After the 1979 Galante murder and the 1981 killing of the three Capos, Massino emerged as the most influential figure in the Bonanno Family, just behind Boss Phil Rastelli.

In January of 1987, Rastelli, Massino, and others were sentenced after being convicted on RICO charges earlier. Rastelli received a variety of judgments with the result he was going to have to do 12 years in the slammer. Massino was hit with ten years. Doing 12 years is not fun but, because of this trial, Rastelli was severed from the Commission case and thus dodged a possible 100-year sentence. Massino would survive his ten years and emerge even more powerful.

Massino and his brother-in-law, Sal Vitale, avoided a big bullet in June of 1987. They were found not guilty of the three Capos murders from May of 1981. Massino's strategy of avoiding the first trial, which resulted in the conviction of Lefty Ruggiero and others, had paid off.

CONCLUSION

While the FBI did an excellent job with the Pizza Connection case, and their netting of Rastelli and Massino et al. for extortion, the Bonanno Family was not decimated and lived to emerge unified and stable in the 1990s.

THE COLOMBO FAMILY

As described earlier in this book, Boss Carmine Persico was in and out of court and in and out of prison all through the seventies and early 1980s. Nevertheless, the FBI set its sights on the Colombo Family in their "Star Quest" investigation.

1982 was the big year. The FBI obtained permission to bug the home of Acting Boss Tom DiBella. Not much was happening there, but it did give them enough evidence to obtain legal grounds to put electronic surveillance into the residence of Dominic "Donny Shacks" Montemarano, a close Persico Associate. In turn, that bug led them to Montemarano's Maniac Club, then to the key spot, the Casa Sorta restaurant. It was there that Acting Boss Gennaro "Gerry Lang" Langella held court. The Colombos would later wish that everyone just ate and didn't say a word. Too late!

On June 13, 1986, much of the leadership of the Colombo Family were found guilty on RICO charges. Among those going down were; Carmine Persico, Gerry Langella, Al Persico Jr., Capo Andy Russo, and others. Their sentences were delayed till after the Commission trail, and they were devastating. Persico was hit with 39 years, Langella got 65 years, Russo received 12, Al Persico Jr. was given 12 years, and the others also weren't happy when the judge was finished. Ralph Scopo and Donny Shacks Montemarano had been severed from the case due to illness but would later receive 15 and 18 years respectively. It was a devastating blow to the leadership.

In addition to the Criminal RICO case, the Colombo Family was a target of a Civil Racketeering offensive aimed to keep them out of Local 6A and the District Council of Concrete and Cement Workers of the Laborers Union. Some Colombo members and associates were banned from the union, but others managed to remain entrenched. This aspect of the attack on the Colombo's would have to be labeled partially successful.

CONCLUSION

Going into the 1986 Commission trial, the feds had severely weakened the hold the Colombo Family had on a critical union racket plus Boss Carmine Persico was realistically looking at spending the rest of his life in prison. The goal for him would soon become one of keeping the throne open until his son, Al Jr., was released from prison. That would mean that there would be bodies in the streets again.

THE GENOVESE FAMILY

In December of 1983, the FBI successfully bugged the Palma Boy's Social Club at 416 East 115th Street in Manhattan. From that point on its primary occupant, Fat Tony Salerno was toast.

From these tapes, and others, the FBI learned a number of things including; information about the "Concrete Club", the Commission's involvement in a Buffalo Family leadership dispute, more details of the Commission and how it related to the Bonanno Family, and the Commission's participation in the election of the leader of the Teamsters Union.

On March 21, 1986, a 29 count RICO indictment came down on the heads of Tony Salerno and 14 others. The defendants were facing RICO conspiracy and RICO violations. Among the predicate acts were; extortion, mail fraud, bookmaking, numbers, conspiracy to rig the Teamsters elections, and a conspiracy to commit murder. This case wouldn't come to trial till after the Commission trial was finished.

BAIL REFORM ACT

In 1984, Congress passed the Bail Reform Act. Essentially it allowed the refusal of bail to a defendant if the government could prove he was a danger to the community. Salerno and his protégé, Vincent "Fish" Cafaro were refused bail in the Genovese Family case. They appealed and won at the Second Court of Appeals. Eventually, the matter went before the Supreme Court of the United States, which upheld the constitutionality of the Bail Reform Act.

CONCLUSION

Electronic surveillance doomed Salerno and some of his underlings. It was not just the evidence from the Palma Boys Social Club, but also tapes from Ralph Scopo's surveillance and other locations. Without the recordings, it is highly unlikely Salerno and others would have been convicted on many charges.

GAMBINO FAMILY

Soldier Angelo Ruggiero was a life-long friend of future Gambino Boss John Gotti. Ruggiero's brother was a big-time heroin dealer. Taps on Ruggiero's phones and then bugs in his new home revealed his deep involvement in dealing drugs. This would lead to Ruggiero and others being jammed up on heroin charges. But these events would also lead to the FBI getting permission to install a bug in the home of Boss Paul Castellano.

PAUL CASTELLANO

Castellano rode the coattails of his brother-in-law, Carlo Gambino, to the top of that Family. Before his natural death in 1976, Gambino had been quite ill and looked to Castellano to act in his place. This decision was made easier because long-time Underboss, Neil Dellacroce, was jammed up on legal problems resulting in a prison sentence. A dying Gambino let it be known that it was his desire that Castellano succeeded him. Fortunately for "Big Paul," Dellacroce did not contest this wish.

As Boss of the Gambino Family, Castellano became the primary target of the FBI. They had obtained legal permission to install a bug in his home in March 1983 and succeeded in doing so. Castellano was a dead duck, but he did not know it yet. Castellano was trying to juggle too many balls as the 1980s progressed.

On March 30, 1984, Castellano and 20 others were indicted on a massive RICO case. The counts included 25 murders, car theft, loansharking, drug trafficking and bribery. Fortunately for Castellano, he was indirectly involved in these matters, so he had a chance of beating the charges.

At the same time, Castellano became aware that key members of Capo John Gotti's crew had been arrested for drug dealing. Most of the evidence came from electronic surveillance of the Ruggiero home. Castellano wanted transcripts of these conversations so he could make his own judgment whether this group had broken the Commission rule against drug dealers. His real reason was that he was hoping to be able to decimate the Gotti crew so Gotti would not be a contender for his throne, in the event Castellano had to go to prison.

The Commission indictment came down on February 25, 1985. Castellano was arrested once again and needed a significant sum to bail himself out. A month later, Underboss Neil Dellacroce, John Gotti, and other members of his crew were indicted on RICO charges including loansharking, gambling, and hijacking. Most of the top players in the Family were facing the possibility of prison time. Both groups started planning for that eventuality.

THE HIT

For some reason, Castellano procrastinated on taking a decisive step against Gotti and his crew. That would prove to be fatal. Gotti had been busy. He had gained the support of many Gambino Family powers and up and coming mobsters like Sammy "The Bull" Gravano. This group had also carefully felt out some of the second line leaders in the Bonanno, Colombo, and Lucchese Families. Gotti et al. felt they had the green light to take out Castellano.

Supposed Castellano loyalist, Capo Frank DeCicco, betrayed his Boss and let the Gotti crew know when Castellano would be attending a meeting in a Manhattan restaurant. Four men were assigned to gun down Castellano and his new Underboss, Tom Bilotti. Three other men were in backup positions. Gotti and Gravano were sitting in a car just down the street as observers and backup shooters if necessary.

Castellano and Bilotti were killed as they exited their vehicle on December 16, 1985. Castellano's legal problems were over. So were those of Underboss Neil Dellacroce, who had passed away on December 2, of the same year. There would be no Gambino Family members as defendants in the Commission trial.

CONCLUSION

These FBI investigations of the Gambino Family did not go in a straight line. New charges were added, others dropped, and further possible defendants came into the picture, while others faded for one reason or another. However, the goal was never forgotten. It was to decimate the leadership of the Gambino Family. This was accomplished, but it wasn't the Commission case that achieved this goal.

THE LUCCHESE FAMILY

The bravery of Long Island garbage men Robert Kubecka and Donald Barstow played a role in the destruction of the Lucchese Family leadership of the 1980s. They refused to buckle under to the attempts to kick their company into going along with the garbage cartel that was being run by Capo Sal Avellino. In June of 1982, Kubecka and Barstow made the fateful decision to operate undercover for a New York State Task Force. Convictions were obtained but despite assurances from the Task Force that they and their families would be safe, Kubecka and Barstow were murdered.

THE JAGUAR

Avellino's home was bugged then his beautiful Jaguar. The Task Force had hit a gold mine. From March 1983 through July 1983, the passengers in Avellino's vehicle talked themselves and others into prison.

Boss Anthony Corallo was frequently in the Jaguar. He and Avellino talked about a variety of topics including the existence of the Commission, disputes involving the Commission, the Concrete Club, and a host of other illegal matters. Underboss Salvatore Santoro also was taped in Avellino's chariot talking about Joe Bonanno's book, which outlined the formation and operation of the Commission. The good guys also learned about upcoming meetings that they could monitor and the opinions the Lucchese leaders had of the other Commission members. The take from the Jaguar tapes was priceless.

GOODFELLAS

Martin Scorcese made a great film, "Goodfellas," based on Nicholas Pileggi's story about Lucchese Associate Henry Hill. Paul Vario was the real-life leader of the crew that Hill was aligned with. On April 3, 1984, Vario was sentenced to four years for providing a no-show job for Hill when he was released from prison.

On February 21, 1985, just before the Commission indictment, Vario and ten others were arrested on RICO charges involving extortion and attempted extortion of freight companies at JFK airport. Eventually, Vario would be given a ten-year sentence. It completed a lousy decade for Vario with seemingly endless courtroom battles and periodic prison terms. He was no longer a factor in the Family.

CHAPTER SEVENTEEN

The Commission Defendants: Part One

CARMINE "JUNIOR" PERSICO

It would really take a book to tell the incredible story of Carmine Persico. What follows will only be a short summary of his life.

Persico was born between older sibling Alphonse and youngest brother Theodore. All three of them would spend their lives within the milieu of LCN. There was also a sister named Delores.

By the 1950s, the two older Persico brothers were ricocheting around Brooklyn and periodically coming to the attention of the police. In May of 1950, Carmine was arrested after one man was killed and another stabbed in a gang fight. Eventually, the charges were dropped.

Nearly a year later, in February of 1951, a Steve Bove was killed. Carmine Persico was arrested and charged with murder two weeks later. Not long afterward, older brother Alphonse turned himself in, and Carmine was released. Early in September, Al began serving a twenty-year sentence on the Bove murder. Which of the two actually killed Bove remains murky.

Carmine's next arrest happened on May 25, 1952. He was with powerful gambling czar Frank "Frankie Shots" Abbatemarco and Joey Gallo when they are rounded up by the NYPD. As was discussed in a previous chapter, Gallo would be involved in killing Abbatemarco in 1959. What this arrest demonstrated was that Persico, like Gallo, was most likely acting as a collector for Frankie Shot's gambling operation.

THE BIG HURT

Unknowingly, Persico would put a millstone around his neck with a simple hijacking. On July 28, 1959, an Ackers Motor Lines truck, full of linen, was hijacked. Persico and his crew were quickly arrested. This set off a long series of trials, appeals, and retrials, which plagued him for decades. One of the results of this legal quagmire was that it prevented Persico from openly taking the throne in 1971 when Boss Joe Colombo was wounded.

THE GALLO WAR

Between 1961 and the end of 1963, the so-called Gallo War sporadically raged on the streets of Brooklyn. According to what Carmine Persico told Joe Valachi, at first, most of the soldiers were in revolt against Boss Joe Profaci. Eventually many drifted away from the Gallos who were at the heart of the upheaval. Persico and his crew not only left the Gallos but became Profaci's spearhead against them. There were countless incidents, but we will focus on those that directly involved Persico. During this period Persico was in an out of court on his hijacking problem.

Rebel Larry Gallo surprisingly accepted an invitation from John Scimone to meet at the Sahara Lounge in Queen's New York on August 20, 1961. Scimone was with the opposing forces, and younger brother Albert urged Larry not to go. He did and was the worse for wear for doing so.

At the bar, Gallo was jumped and nearly garrotted to death. Only the entry of a curious police officer saved his life. The assailants, one of them being Carmine Persico, fled and escaped. Of course, Gallo knew who had tried to kill him but Commission rules forbad him from identifying them to the cops.

Gallo fudged the rule a little. He signed a statement that acknowledged that the police officers involved in the incident had identified Persico as one of the assailants. It was likely Larry was sending a message that he knew who tried to kill him. Everyone knew retaliation was coming. The question was when.

BOMBS AWAY

There were many violent episodes in the Gallo War. Two specifically involved Carmine Persico and were described in Chapter Fifteen. He survived a bombing in January of 1963 and on May 19, 1963, lived despite being severely wounded by gunfire.

ENDLESS COURTROOMS

Persico's seemly endless legal entanglement around a 1959 hijacking case is mentioned above. It wasn't the only legal problem Persico had. He and others had been indicted for assaulting a Gallo associate in the famous Copacabana Night Club in early 1962. He was in and out of court on that charge. Eventually, a sentence of two weeks was levied in March of 1968. As usual, Persico was freed on bail while appealing his conviction.

AFTER THE WAR

The Gallo War petered out when Joe Colombo became the new Boss in 1964. It would be logical to think that Persico would take a break after years of stress but that would be wrong. Not only did Persico have to continue to fight his many court cases but the money had to be found to pay his high priced attorneys. Making money in the mob often ruffled feathers. Persico made someone angry.

From information supplied by secret informer Greg Scarpa, the FBI learned that Boss Joe Colombo has put out a hit contract on someone who had threatened Persico. The contract, according to Scarpa, was given to Frank Locicero. Unfortunately, there is no follow up information as to who the target was. Years later, Locicero would be part of the hit team that finally killed Joey Gallo.

Then Persico was arrested on loansharking charges. The next day, February 28, 1969, the New York Times reported that this was Persico's 24th arrest in 18 years. Persico made the same paper in June when they stated that Persico was a regular at a bar owned by famous New York Jet quarterback Joe Namath. In September he was arrested for harassing a cop who was ticketing his brother for a parking violation. With Persico, trouble never seemed to end.

BROTHER AL

There was some good news for Carmine. His older brother Al had begun a 20-year sentence for murder in 1951. In October of 1967, Alphonse won a sentence reduction and was released that November. This would be very important for Carmine would be in an out of the slammer over the next 15 years. Al would be there to hold down the fort. He would ensure that the Persicos continued to rule the Colombo Family with an iron fist.

MORE TROUBLE

Fred DeLuca was a long-time member of the Persico crew. Suddenly, on November 20, 1969, his family reported him missing. The FBI started poking around and pumping their informants for any news on what was going on. They soon learned that Sal "Sally D" D'Ambrosia had fallen off the map as well. This jumped the mystery up a considerable number of notches. The D'Ambrosias were very tight with Persico. Brother Al D'Ambrosia had been in Persico's car and was wounded when the Gallos put three slugs into Carmine back in 1963. Something serious was up.

It didn't take long for the FBI to figure out that D'Ambrosia and DeLuca were dead. The word on the street was that the two were beginning to talk and act somewhat independently. If you are going to survive in LCN, rivals, have to be dealt with swiftly and mercilessly. In street talk, D'Ambrosia and DeLuca were "gone" which meant they were dead and never coming back. No proof emerged that Persico had the murders committed. However, it is hard to imagine anyone would kill two close Associates of his in an independent move.

THE BIG BREAK

Joe Colombo had been Boss of the Family since 1964. At first, he was basically unknown but as the FBI realized his status, the pressure increased, and it got under his skin. In a story that has been retold countless times, Colombo became a household name and even appeared on the famous Dick Cavett TV talk show. Here's a brief summary of his rise and fall.

The straw that broke the camel's back for Colombo was when his son, Joseph Jr. was arrested for melting down silver coins. The silver was worth far more than the face value of the currency. Ironically, this case fell apart later, but at the time Colombo went berserk.

He quickly gathered up a number of his minions and began picketing the FBI's New York headquarters claiming prejudice against Italian-Americans. The protest took off culminating in a giant rally at Columbus Circle on June 29, 1970. Seeing the numbers that Colombo drew, the politicians and others began folding like decks of cards. Unbelievably, US Attorney John Mitchell (a crook) banned the use of the word Mafia and New York State governor Nelson Rockefeller quickly followed suit. It was madness.

Not surprisingly the FBI responded by increasing pressure on all the New York Families and especially Colombo himself. Soon informers were reporting great misgivings about Colombo's pseudo-civil-rights strategy. The discontent even moved into his inner circle. Worse yet, his long-time mentor, Carlo Gambino, arguably the most powerful Boss in New York, withdrew his support. Gambino felt Colombo's campaign was causing too much heat. Colombo ignored him as the second rally was about to take place.

On June 28, 1971, Colombo was gunned down by a lone nut shooter who was then quickly dispatched by Colombo Associate Philip Rosillo. Some theories emerged as to whether the hit was a conspiracy. This is not the place to discuss those ideas. Colombo was incapacitated and would die seven years later.

BEHIND THE SCENES

In the confusion after Colombo was shot, the Family needed interim leadership till the smoke cleared. Consigliere Joseph "Joe Yack" Yacovelli appointed easily manipulated Vinny Aloi as Acting Boss. Informant Joe Luparelli later said Aloi was selected because, "…Junior (Persico) was about to go to the can so he wouldn't be able to control the Family." In actuality, Persico was running the Family, but he knew a prison sentenced loomed so having "formal" leaders in place was important.

BYE BYE JOEY

As the confusion eased after the Colombo shooting, it slowly became clear that Joey Gallo had nothing to do with the hit. Nevertheless, he had been and would most likely continue to be a monster irritation to the Colombo Family and by extension to Carlo Gambino. Joe Luparelli related how he drove Consigliere Joe Yacovelli to a Commission meeting. According to Luparelli, Joe Yack was elated when he emerged. "Joe Yack told me all the Commission had approved the contract on Gallo." Luparelli later related. Now it was just a matter of time.

In Charles Brandt's hugely successful book, "I Hear You Paint Houses," Teamster Frank Sheeran claimed that he had shot Joey Gallo. It was a ridiculous boast that was quickly demolished by forensic and eyewitness testimony. The truth is that it was just bad luck that did Gallo in. Below is a brief summary of his death on April 7, 1972.

Gallo, his wife, his stepdaughter, Peter Diapoulos, and Pete's girlfriend, went looking for a place to eat after an evening at the Copacabana. They intended to go to Chinatown to Su Lings but found it closed. Gallo insisted on looking for another place instead of going home as Diapoulos suggested. They eventually came upon the newly opened, "Umberto's Clam House" and went in. Unfortunately, they had been spotted. It was pure luck.

Joseph Luparelli, a mob Associate, saw the Gallo party arrive. He just happened to be standing outside Umberto's. Luparelli immediately rushed a few blocks south to a joint where he had previously been drinking with Carmine "Sonny Pinto" DiBiase, a wild Genovese Family member. Upon hearing the news of Gallo's nearby presence, one of them called Colombo Consigliere Joe Yacovelli for orders. He told them to kill Gallo immediately.

DiBiase, Frank "Cisco" Locicero, and Benjamin "Benny" Locicero drove up to Umberto's in DiBiase's vehicle. Luparelli and Phil "Fat Fungy" Gambino were in Luparelli's car which they used to block traffic at the site. DiBiase, Cisco, and Benny charged in the side door of Umberto's and unloaded their guns at Gallo. Crazy Joey desperately attempted to flee out the front door. He collapsed in the street mortally wounded. The three gunman raced out the side door followed by shots fired at them by Diapoulos. They escaped. Crazy Joey Gallo was dead but would live on in legend.

SIGNIFICANCE OF THE GALLO HIT

Gallo had been a pain in the rear for three Colombo Bosses, Joe Profaci, Joe Magliocco, and Joe Colombo. Carmine Persico would not have to deal with this wildcard. He was in prison on his hijacking sentence when the killing went down and thus avoided the inevitable Gallo retaliation attempts. Later, an internal Gallo feud led to some murders, which were ended by the approved separate hits on John "Mooney" Cutrone, and Gennaro Basciano. They had ignored the Commission edict to stop the feuding. Peace had finally come to the Colombo Family and Carmine Persico was holding all the strings.

ACTING BOSSES

Most experts on LCN agree that after the wounding of Colombo in 1971, Carmine Persico became the most powerful member of that Family. The questions as to exactly when he became the official Boss would remain important up to the present day.

Consigliere Joe "Joe Yack" Yacovelli first appointed Capo Vinnie Aloi as Acting Boss. Aloi's reign did not last long. He got jammed up with legal problems and was replaced by veteran Capo Tom DiBella. Informant Greg Scarpa, in July of 1973, reported DiBella's elevation. Other informants put the date as December of 1972.

In 1974, DiBella was briefly replaced as Acting Boss by Capo John Brancato. DiBella was doing a short prison sentence. But by October 31, 1975, DiBella was back in the saddle as he performed the induction ceremony of Michael Franzese and others.

STILLBIRTH REVOLT

In 1977, Underboss Tony Abbatemarco (son of Frankie Shots) and veteran member Salvatore "Sally" Albanese, staged a mini-revolt. They complained to the Commission about the behavior of Consigliere Alphonse "Allie Boy" Persico. Their claims were totally rejected, which meant they were in big trouble. In June, informer Joe Cantaluppo recorded a member saying that "Sally Albanese was gone." That meant he was dead. Miraculously, Abbatemarco was able to or was allowed to flee. (He died in anonymity in 2005)

OFFICIAL BOSS

During a pre-sentence hearing for Alphonse "Allie Boy" Persico, on June 20, 1980, informer Joe Cantaluppo testified that Carmine Persico was the Boss of the Colombo Family. That claim was supported by November 5, 1980, FBI report that stated informer Greg Scarpa had indicated that Carmine Persico was the official Boss and that the Commission had approved this change. (DiBella voluntarily stepped down)

Since Persico was still in prison, yet another Acting Boss had to be selected. Underboss Jerry Langella was tapped to be the new stand-in. When Persico was released in March of 1984, Langella moved back to his Underboss position yet he continued to represent the Family at Commission meetings. Carmine Persico didn't want another parole violation.

ALLEGED KILLINGS

It is an understood fact of life in LCN that fear of violence and violence are critical instruments to keep the troops in line. It was no different in the Colombo Family. Some hits took place which informants placed at the feet of Persico. Since he was never charged in any of these murders, the claims of the informants must remain as allegations, not fact.

Informer Sal Misciotta stated that Persico approved the killing of a man in the winter of 1978. Misciotta and Jimmy Angelino were the shooters with John Minerva driving the hit car. According to Misciotta, Michael Franzese picked up that hit team after they abandoned their vehicle.

Notorious informer Greg Scarpa told the FBI that Persico had signed off on some killings. He listed; the 1980 hit on Gerry Pappa, the August 26/80 murder of Dominic Somma, the January 1981 shooting of Nicolas Prospero, and the March 1982, murder of John Matera. Scarpa was often a liar and extremely devious. His claims have to be treated cautiously.

BRIBERY

Carmine Persico knew his way around the prison system. Early in 1973, he was hauled into court because of the alleged favors he was receiving in food and phone privileges. When the judge wondered aloud whether Persico might corrupt the whole jail the Special U.S. Attorney responded, "It's not that he could, he is presently doing so." The judge thought it best if Persico was sent off to the supermaxim prison in Marion, Illinois.

Four years later, Persico was languishing in Atlanta prison on his hijacking sentence. He and some of his men thought they had their hooks into a corrupt IRS agent. They started out slowly by paying the agent to have Persico moved to New York for a few days so he could see his wife and some friends. Persico was then returned back to Atlanta positive that he was on to a good thing.

Then Persico, through others, paid to be moved to New York for the Christmas holidays. The long-range plan was to gain an early release from his sentence. On February 2, 1978, Persico was taped saying to the IRS agent, "We'll love you for this if you make it good." Unfortunately for Persico, the IRS agent was playing a double game. Persico eventually pled out to conspiracy to bribe and was given a five-year sentence in November of 1981.

As unbelievable as it may sound, Persico was right back in the business of manipulating the prison system. This time he fell victim to a sting run by the FBI. They were using Gambino Associate Joseph "Joe Dogs" Iannuzzi, as an informer. The FBI had successfully fooled some of Persico's underlings into believing that Iannuzzi had a powerful connection in Washington. To prove this, they arranged for a Colombo soldier to be placed in a prison of his choice. When word of this backdoor deal got around to Persico, he and his men, were eager to use the same connection.

For some reason, Persico's men were slow in coming up with the $20,000 that they were told was the bribe amount needed. Finally, the Bureau of Prisons moved the original "winner" of the bribery scam. Persico was quickly transferred to a prison in California. He was desperate for Iannuzzi's connection to get him back to the east so he could continue to run his Family. It didn't happen.

MORE LEGAL PROBLEMS

In March of 1984, Carmine Persico was released from prison. In October of the same year, he and a host of other Colombo members were arrested in what would become the Colombo Family Trial. At this point, Persico got into the wind. Thanks to an informer he and Don "Donny Shacks" Montemarano were found and arrested. Two years later, Persico was convicted in the Colombo Family Trial and then was later sentenced to 39 years. Meanwhile, he was indicted in the Commission case, and he was in a world of hurt.

PERSONALITY

Michael Franzese was a Capo during the Persico regime and interacted with him on some occasions. In his book, "Quitting the Mob" Franzese wrote "He (Persico) was a tough, gritty man who stood five feet seven and ate, drank, and slept the Mob. He was comfortable with the violence… murder was a vital cog in the business machinery of the Mob."

These observations from Franzese provide the reader some insight into the personality of the man who would roll the dice and defend himself in the Commission trial.

CHAPTER EIGHTEEN

The Commission Defendants: Part Two

ANTHONY "FAT TONY" SALERNO

Salerno was born in the Bronx, NY, on August 15, 1911. Like many members of LCN, as a youngster, Salerno was labeled "incorrigible." But it wasn't until the 1940's that his name appeared on police blotters. These were minor charges, one in Rhode Island, the other in Miami that amounted to nothing.

JOE VALACHI

Famous turncoat Joe Valachi didn't have much to say about Salerno but what he did was interesting. In the 1930's, Valachi had been ordered to beat up two brothers, members of the Lucchese Family, for some transgression. Valachi was married to a daughter of a former Boss of the Lucchese Family and was very friendly with the then Underboss, Tom Lucchese.

Valachi didn't want to take any chances of ruining his relationship with Lucchese. His original inclination was to pretend he couldn't find the victims. That tactic didn't work for Salerno phoned Valachi and explained that he was to meet one of the victims at a specific place and time, the next day. Valachi was trapped. The beating was administered and, just as Valachi feared, Lucchese and his men were not happy. Fortunately for Valachi, his friendship with Lucchese saved him.

BOXING

It took a major heavyweight boxing fight in 1959 to propel Salerno into the limelight. At the time, Floyd Patterson had been World Champion for three years after winning the title by defeating the legendary Archie Moore. Ingemar Johansson, of Sweden, was the number one contender and the natural opponent for Patterson's next title defense.

Johansson defeated Patterson on June 26, 1959, to win the crown but lost two subsequent title matches in the following years. The outcome of the fight was not the story, but the financing of it was. The information that follows originated from various investigations that ensued in the wake of rumors that the mob was involved in the fight.

William Rosenshon was a neophyte promotor with big ideas. He was able to sign Johansson to the first title contest, but there was a clause that limited Rosenshon to forty days to sign champion Patterson. If that was not done, Rosenshon was out $10,000. (Approximately $83,000 today). He was up against it.

According to Rosenshon's later testimony, Patterson's manager, Gus D'Amato, refused to sign the deal unless Salerno and a man named Charles Antonucci were brought in on the promotion. At that point, Rosenshon meet with Salerno. He agreed to front $25,000 for the promotion plus give Rosenshon $10,000 for expenses. The kicker was that one-third of the profits would go to Salerno and another third to Antonucci, who operated under the name Black.

District Attorney Frank Hogan told the press that Rosenshon explained that Salerno brought Vincent J. Valella in as front man for the interests of him and Antonucci. Valella, a local attorney, and politician, vehemently denied he was fronting for anyone. Valella stated that the $25,000 came from his savings. He also threatened to sue Rosenshon for $5,000,000. Nothing happened with that.

Eventually, D'Amato lost his New York State license to be a boxing manager or to act as an aid (called a "second") in the ring. Rosenshon matchmaker's license was suspended for three years. On December 10, 1959, Valella was charged with two counts of perjury connected to his testimony on these convoluted affairs before the New York State Athletic Commission and a grand jury. Salerno avoided testifying by remaining in Miami. The publicity must have been unwelcome, and surely he didn't like to be referred to as "a person of ill repute," but there was no long-term damage to his mob career.

PLAYING THE NUMBERS

Salerno made his fortune running a vast numbers operation in Harlem in New York City. It had fallen into the lap of the Genovese Family after they killed the famous "Dutch" Shultz in 1935. One of Salerno's Soldiers, Vincent "Fish" Cafaro, testified that in a good year, his operation, a part of Salerno's, would result in a profit of $2,000,000, which he would split with Salerno.

That was tax-free money pouring into Fat Tony's pocket. The Fish's operation was just a part of Salerno's illegal sources for cash. An indictment, released on May 3, 1977, charged that Salerno and others took in, "at least $10 million annually in illegal policy (numbers) wagers in Manhattan." That's approximately $41,400,000 in today's dollars!

For non-street people, the question follows, "What is a numbers operation?" Below is a very simplified example of this lucrative racket.

One:
A gambler pays $1 and selects the number 234. Nine hundred and ninety-nine others are also placing their $1 bets the same day. The total "take" is $1000.

Two:
"Runners" pick up all the bets and the money and take them to a "Bank" where the money would be counted and the bets organized.

Three:
At the end of the day, a race track would announce the total amount of money bet on three separate categories: wins (first), places (second), and shows (third).

Four:
Imagine those figures were: $3456 bet on winners that day, $2987 bet on all the horses that came in second, and $1874 bet on all the third place horses.

Five:
The winning number would be 674, the last digit in each of the three categories listed above.

Six:
This number would be totally random, and thus the players would believe the number wasn't fixed.

Seven:
The winning number was readily available in the newspaper.

Eight:
The next day the "Banker" would send runners out to not only collect that day's bets but to pay those who had the winning number.

Nine:
Imagine there was only one winning better and the total wagered was $1000. The "winner" would be paid $600 leaving $400 in gross profit for the operator of the numbers operation.

This racket can't be successfully operated unless the local police ignore it. For that to happen, payoffs have to be made to law enforcement at various levels and often to powerful politicians. Corruption was rampant in New York City and elsewhere back in the day. A quick read of the books "Serpico" and "Prince of the City" will provide insight into that era.

LOAN SHARKING

Gambling and loansharking go hand in hand. The gambling generates illegal profits, which cannot be placed in a bank account. Instead, it is loaned out to those who can't borrow money from legitimate institutions for their credit is usually beyond pathetic. Not surprisingly, the interest rates are very high. If someone borrowed $5, he owed $6 in seven days. That doesn't seem like much but read on.

On May 30, 1973, Salerno and others were indicted for running a loan-sharking operation that had, "$80,000,000 in loans on the street in one day." That is $454,000,000 today. No small change even if the numbers are highly inflated. Assistant DA John Fine told the press that Salerno,

"Controls organized loan sharking and gambling in New York and Florida." The indictment claimed that Salerno's operation charged 3% a week or 156% a year. It would be effortless to fall behind with payments at those rates.

LIFESTYLE

During his adult life, Salerno split his time between three places. He always had a Manhattan apartment, where he would bed down at night during the week. On weekends he would most often be found at his country home near Reinbeck, New York. During the winter, Salerno moved to Miami Beach, although he was often in and out of New York City as business required.

At the Reinbeck estate, Salerno had an indoor riding barn built to accommodate the horse riding interests of his only daughter. She would marry in the early 1960's and would produce Salerno's first grandchild. There is no indication that Salerno loved the nightlife in his later years although that may have been true in his youth.

PERSONALITY

Thanks to a couple of brief interviews that Salerno gave we have a small insight into his personality. When a reporter spoke to him in a courthouse, Salerno said, "They had everyone down here on me. They say I hid $100,000 over four years." When the reporter complimented Salerno on how well he was dressed, the Mafioso responded, "They say I got so much money. How could I come dressed like a bum?" After that, Salerno made some disparaging comments on Italian cops and how Serpico had ruined cops ability to do business. Finally, Salerno spoke words that probably also applied nearly a decade later, when he was facing the Commission charges. "If they wanted to get me why didn't they do it when I was younger? What the hell do I want with jail now?" Salerno lamented.

We get another insight into Salerno thanks to the brilliant New York writer and columnist Jimmy Breslin. He accidentally ran into Fat Tony on the street in Harlem and wrote a piece about their encounter on January 19, 1980.

Breslin inquired of Salerno as to whether he'd be attending the upcoming Super Bowl. To this Salerno replied, "The parole officer says I'm not supposed to be with any known names. What am I going to do? I don't know anybody who is unknown. So I stay here on the corner."

Another example comes from an FBI report. An agent spoke to Salerno, in a Federal Court building about what he was doing there. Salerno explained that he had appeared before a Federal Grand Jury but took the 5th instead of answering questions about gambling. He went on to say that Joe Valachi, the famous informer, was nuts and his whole family was nuts. Then Salerno brushed over his mob career by saying that he had been a gambler all his life. Apparently, to Salerno, this wasn't something terrible.

Finally, during the Commission trial, Fat Tony Salerno was no longer pretending to be amazed that the government was after him for gambling, He was resigned to his fate. Someone offered the sugar-loving Salerno a granola bar and suggested it would be better for his health. According to FBI Agent Jules Bonavalonta, Salerno replied, "Who the fuck cares. I am going to die in the fucking can, anyway." He got that right.

MURDER

Salerno was not noted to be a killer but, in LCN, death is a fact of life. Informers provided the FBI with information that Fat Tony was involved with three hits.

Famous informer, Jimmy "The Weasel" Fratianno testified, that he was present at a meeting of the Genovese Family administration, when Salerno, the Consigliere, and the others, voted for a hit on a Joseph Ullo. (It never happened)

Former Philadelphia Underboss Philip Leonetti also connected Salerno to a murder. In 1980, Philadelphia Consigliere, Antony "Tony Bananas" Caponigro, successfully completed a coup that killed Philadelphia Boss Angelo Bruno. The Commission quickly ordered an investigation, which was undertaken by the Genovese Family. Caponigro was brought before the Genovese administration, which included Salerno.

According to Leonetti, Salerno and the others voted to kill Caponigro and anyone involved with him in the plot. Caponigro ended up dead in the trunk of a car. Other bodies soon followed.

It should be mentioned that Salerno's close associate, Vincent "Fish" Cafaro, had a different take on the Caponigro killing. Fish told a Senate Committee that Caponigro first came to Salerno but, Salerno then sent him to see Vincent "Chin" Gigante, the real power in the family in 1980. Whatever Salerno's involvement, Caponigro and the others still ended up dead.

Leonettti also wrote that Salerno was part of the Genovese administration that sat in judgment of Philadelphia Underboss Pete Casella in 1981. Casella had arranged the bombing death of Philadelphia Boss Phil Testa, who had only been in power for a year. For some reason, Casella was spared the death sentence and banished to Florida.

At that point, Leonetti's uncle, Nicky Scarfo, became the new Boss. He arranged the deaths of others connected to the bombings. It can be assumed that the Genovese administration, including Salerno, gave their blessings for these hits, but that conclusion has to remain in the area of speculation.

From the evidence above and knowledge of life in LCN, it is fair to say that Salerno was no stranger to death as a means to keep order.

POSITION

In the 1985 Commission indictment, Salerno was identified as the Boss of the Genovese Family. He was not and never had been. We do know he was inducted into the family at some point and became a Capo around 1963. Hidden Boss Phil Lombardo appointed Salerno as his Consigliere in 1972. When Underboss/Acting Boss Frank Tieri was overwhelmed with legal problems and ill health, in 1978, Salerno was moved up to Underboss. It was at this point that he began playing the role of the "Front Boss," to continue keeping real Boss, Phil Lombardo, in the shadows.

Salerno was Acting Boss from 1978 into 1984. However, the truth is a bit more complicated. In 1981, Phil Lombardo was in the hospital when powerful Capo, Vincent "Chin" Gigante, and Consigliere, Bobby Manna informed Lombardo that he was no longer Boss. (It is possible that Lombardo had had enough and it was he who decided to resign.) Gigante and Manna then visited Salerno, who was in the same facility, after suffering a stroke. Salerno was told that he was now only a Soldier, with no authority. Unfortunately, we do not know his thoughts on this demotion.

According to Fish Cafaro, Salerno then went to his summer retreat to recuperate. He became bored and asked Gigante for permission to move back to New York. Gigante decided that Lombardo's hidden Boss tactic might work for him, so he not only allowed Salerno to move back to the Big Apple but also to continue playing the role of "Boss." By this time, all the Bosses in the five New York mob Families knew the real power was Gigante.

CONCLUSION

It was all downhill for Salerno in the 1980s. He had suffered a stroke and had been demoted to Soldier. Then came the overpowering Commission indictment, followed by another that focused strictly on the Genovese Family. He had only done a six month stretch in prison after pleading out on a gambling and tax case back in 1978. The stakes were much higher when he faced trial in 1986. Fat Tony was in huge trouble.

CHAPTER NINETEEN

The Commission Defendants: Part Three

ANTONIO "TONY DUCKS" CORALLO

Corallo was born in New York City on February 2, 1913. By the time he was an adult, he was 5 feet 7 inches and weighed in at about 170 pounds. Corallo had two brothers and three sisters, none of whom achieved the infamy of Tony Ducks.

A Bureau of Narcotics report from the early 1960s stated that Corallo had an extensive arrest record beginning in 1929. They listed; grand larceny, robbery, and violation of the New York State Narcotic Law. This last arrest resulted in a six-month term for Corallo, which was the norm around that time. Clearly, he was not convicted on most of the 12 charges laid against him.

Although there is no primary source, the legend is that Corallo got the nickname, "Tony Ducks" because he "ducked" so many charges. Whether that is a true story is irrelevant. He was always going to be "Tony Ducks" including in the newspaper reports when he passed away.

UNION TROUBLE

Corallo became well known in the 1950's for his activities with various unions. He was part of a large group who were pushing Jimmy Hoffa for Teamsters General President. As one small part of the plan, Hoffa wanted to gain control of the New York area Joint Council. It was composed of about 57 locals. The executive board of the Joint Council was elected by the members of the local executive boards. It follows then that the more locals Hoffa controlled, the better his chances of managing the Joint Council.

With the help of Corallo and John "Johnny Dio" Dioguardi, Hoffa was able to get six New York area, non-Teamsters locals, recognized as Teamsters locals and thus their executive boards would be able to vote in Joint Council elections. Not surprisingly Hoffa's opponents raised a fuss, and the noise was so loud that it attracted the attention of politicians and various District Attorneys.

In March of 1956, famed District Attorney Frank Hogan went to the media with his concerns about the election of the Joint Council. His Assistant DA, Alfred J. Scotti, told the press that Corallo and Dioguardi were spearheading the underworlds drive to control the New York area Teamsters. He made a note of the chartering of the six locals in time for the February 14, 1956 election that remained in legal dispute for some time afterward. Mr. Scotti described Corallo as, "One of the most powerful underworld figures in the field of labor."

The uproar over the contested Teamsters Joint Council election continued into the next year. Dave Beck, the embattled General President of the Teamsters, sent a trustee into New York to oust the puppet leaders of the six locals connected to Corallo and Dioguardi. He did nothing.

A Senate committee was formed to investigate the multiple problems in the unions and management. Corallo was called to testify on August 15, 1959. He was uncooperative and sullen, taking the 5th Amendment against self-incrimination a total of 120 times. Corallo didn't jump out of the screen as a "star," but he was now a known figure to those in New York involved in construction and the garment industry. This didn't hurt his effectiveness at all.

MAKING MONEY WITH THE UNIONS

Corallo was pulling down a multitude of salaries from various unions including Teamster Local 239, of which Corallo was Vice President. According to Assistant DA Scotti, Corallo controlled six other locals in a variety of industries.

Not all of these were Teamsters locals. For example, on September 12, 1957, the United Textile Workers of America suspended the officers of their Local 229 and put a trustee in charge. The union claimed that the president of the local was a puppet of Corallo. Tony Ducks was in deep with the unions, pulling down huge sums from legal salaries, kickbacks, extortions, and outright stealing from pension funds and the like.

BRIBERY ONE

For Corallo, the sixties might very well be labeled, "The decade of the bribe." The following examples explain why.

Corallo was in the headlines on December 7, 1961, when he and others were arrested in a sensational bribery case. It was alleged that Corallo was part of a conspiracy to bribe New York Supreme Court Justice J. Vincent Keogh and former Assistant DA Elliot Kahaner.

They were supposed to secretly contact a federal judge who was hearing a bankruptcy fraud case involving people known to Corallo. Hopefully, the judge would dismiss charges against four men and give suspended sentences to three others. The plot failed when the word got to the judge, and the cops were called in.

In June, Corallo, Keogh, and Kahaner were all convicted. Four months later each received a sentence of two years. A series of appeals followed but when the US Supreme Court refused to review the case they were all off to the slammer.

BRIBERY TWO

Corallo's next bribery case was even more significant than the first. This time it involved a member of the administration of the extremely popular New York Mayor John Lindsey, elected in 1965. This was huge news.

James L. Marcus was New York's Water Commissioner and a poor investor. He got jammed up financially and turned to a loan shark. One thing led to another, and suddenly Marcus was dealing with Corallo. Then Marcus did something even stupider. He agreed to use his influence to win lucrative construction contracts for firms friendly with Corallo, in return for bribes.

Things blew up quickly. On December 22, 1967, Marcus, Corallo, and others were indicted. The allegation was that Marcus ensured that the $ 835,000 (nearly $6 million today) contract to clean the Jerome Park Water Reservoir was awarded to a firm connected to Corallo. It was a no-brainer that the firm would then give Corallo a nice kickback for his services.

On July 26, 1968, Corallo was convicted of conspiracy to bribe and was given a three-year sentence. Judge Edward Weinfeld commented about Corallo, "His entire life reflected a pattern of anti-social conduct from early youth." The Judge went on to say, "It is fairly clear that his income derived from illicit activities-bookmaking, gambling, shylocking (loan sharking) and questionable union activities." It sounded like the Weinfeld was not too impressed by Corallo.

BRIBERY THREE

This case was basically a continuation of the mess with Marcus. Corallo was charged with conspiracy to bribe Marcus in a contract with Consolidated Edison that fell under Marcus' domain as New York Water Commissioner.

Corallo was convicted in December 1969 and was sentenced to 4 ½ years the following February. Luckily for him, the two sentences would run concurrently (at the same time) and thus Corallo was really only facing another year and a half added on to his original three years.

POSITION

It is not sure when Corallo was inducted into the Lucchese Family although the 1950s would be a good guess. Using a series of FBI files as the source, Corallo became a Capo in 1963 at the age of fifty. When Tommy Lucchese died of natural causes in 1967, Corallo was among the leading contenders to replace him. The other candidates basically self-destructed with legal problems. However, Corallo was hamstrung with his bribery charges. The result was that Capo Carmine "Mr. Gibbs "Tramunti became the Boss.

When Corallo was released in the early 1970s, the way was clear for him to take the throne uncontested. Boss Carmine Tramunti continued to be buried under an avalanche of legal problems. Corallo became the Acting Boss in 1973. Paul Vario, Ettore Cocco, and John Dioguardi were also snowed under fighting off a host of charges ending any hopes they may have had to sit on the throne. Corallo was on top and according to the FBI was designated the formal Boss, when Tramunti died in prison in 1978.

CONCLUSION

Antonio "Tony Ducks" Corallo was a veteran member of La Cosa Nostra. He was well connected to other leaders and had plenty of experience making money by any means possible. However, in the 1980s, he made the biggest mistake of his life and doomed himself to prison until he died.

CHAPTER TWENTY

The Commission Defendants: Part Four

GENNARO "GERRY LANG" LANGELLA

Langella tied himself to the Persico flag early on, and thus it wasn't a big surprise that he accompanied Alphonse "Allie Boy" Persico on a visit to see Carmine Persico in Atlanta Penitentiary on April 5, 1972.

Two days later Joey Gallo was gunned down, and a roundup of the Persico crew began. A grand jury issued a series of subpoenas including one with Langella's name on it.

Gerry Lang's first response was to have the subpoena quashed. That tactic failed on December 19, 1972. The same day, he appeared before the grand jury and was given immunity but still refused to answer questions. That led to an indictment for criminal contempt.

Two years later, after more legal maneuvering, Langella pleaded guilty and was given a five-month sentence. Unbelievably, a series of appeals and other legal tactics ensued till it finally ended with an appeals court ruling against Langella on November 22, 1976.

It would be a logical question to ask why Langella spent many tens of thousands of dollars jumping through all these legal hoops rather than merely doing five months in lockup. The answer is simple if you take a broad look at the goings on in the Persico faction during this period.

Carmine Persico was incarcerated. He needed his men on the street, so he didn't lose control of the Colombo Family. Brother Al was jammed up on charges and was either in and out of court or on the run. Consigliere Joe Yacovelli had finally come in from hiding after the Gallo hit, and he too faced an avalanche of legal problems. Stand in Boss Tom DiBella was given a contempt sentence. The strategy, which necessarily had to change continually, was to keep as many Persico flunkies on the street as possible. Thus Langella fought tooth and nail to do just that despite the cost.

VISITING THE FARM

Not too long after the shooting of Joey Gallo, an informer, probably Greg Scarpa, told the FBI that Alphonse "Allie Boy" Persico and some friends were holed up on the rural farm of Carmine Persico. That location, in Saugerties, NY, was put under observation and among other things, the agents saw Langella taking target practice with a rifle.

Not willing to take the chance the Persico crowd were heading out on a mission to kill Gallos, the FBI stopped two vehicles leaving the farm. Langella was in one accompanied by Allie Boy Persico. Two other hoods were in the second car along with a girlfriend of one of them. Persico was held on an outstanding charge involving a loan application. Langella was charged with having illegal fireworks.

Later that day the FBI filed for a search warrant for the farm calling it a "hideout and arsenal." They also included informant information, (Scarpa again) that the Persico crew had marked five Gallos for death. The warrant was granted, and the farm was searched.

On May 3, 1972, Langella pleaded guilty to possessing fireworks, driving while his license was suspended, and illegal possession of a rifle. He was fined $250 on each count and released.

MASSACRE AT THE NEOPOLITAN NOODLE

On the evening of August 11, 1972, Gerry Langella was at the bar of the Neopolitan Noodle restaurant at 320 East 79th Street in Manhattan. Accompanying him were Allie Boy Persico, Allie Boy Jr, who is Carmine's son, Capo Charles Panarella, and Consigliere Joe Yacovelli (the makeup of the group has different versions). For some reason, their presence was known to the Gallo crew. They were still on a revenge rampage for the killing of Joey Gallo back in April. (A few years later, an informant explained that a member of the Colombo Family would feed the Gallos information as to the whereabouts of the significant Persico players.)

The Persico group was moved to a table and replaced at the bar by four males and their wives. Suddenly, a lone shooter opened up with two .38 pistols, killing two of the men and wounding the other two. It took a few days for the cops to discover that the real targets were the Persicos.

Thanks to Peter "Pete the Greek" Diapoulos, we know for certain that the Gallos were behind the shooting. He described being in one of the Gallo hangouts on President Street that fateful day. He began watching a quiet, intense discussion taking place between Al "Blast" Gallo, Punchy Illiano, Sammy "Sammy the Syrian" Zahrablbam, and Louie "Louie the Syrian" Hubella.

At some point Al Gallo said to Diapoulos, "We got a guy, a good guy, coming in to do a piece of work (killing)." A news radio broadcasted a bulletin about the shooting, and the conspirators were briefly elated. When the names of the victims came over the air, they were stunned. It was not the Persico crew but some innocents. It was a disaster for the families of the killed and wounded and a fiasco for the incompetent Gallos.

A hailstorm of negative publicity rained down on the heads of New York City officials who did the usual by forming a grand jury to look into the massacre. Not surprisingly, although Langella and others were hauled in to testify, no one was ever charged for this horrific event.

POSITION

Langella was inducted into the Colombo Family in 1976. The date of his promotion to Capo is murky. What we do know is that a November 5, 1980, FBI report, updating the latest information from informer Greg Scarpa, stated that Carmine Persico had become the formal Boss of the Family and Langella was appointed Acting Consigliere. Scarpa said both moves were approved by the Commission. In another report, from January 7, 1981, Scarpa informed the FBI that Langella was recently made the Underboss.

These moves were made because Carmine Persico was continuing to have legal problems. He later also got jammed up on a parole violation. Brother Al received an extortion conviction and went on the run. Powerful Capo Charles Panarella also did some jail time. The ship would have been rudderless without Langella stepping in to take charge.

Eventually, Langella was appointed the Acting Boss so that the other Families would realize Langella was acting with the full backing of Persico. This was necessary because of the endless conflicts arising from the construction industry racket. When Persico was briefly out on the street, he didn't dare attend any of the Commission meetings for fear of being violated on his parole.

TROUBLE MOUNTS

On November 1, 1982, Langella pleaded guilty to conspiracy to bribe a public official. Langella had been stung by the good guys. They conned Langella into believing he had gotten away with bribing an IRS official. This person moved Carmine Persico from Atlantic prison to New York, in the summer of 1977, and again in December. As usual, Langella was out on the streets while awaiting sentencing.

Unbeknownst to Langella, the FBI had bugged his favorite restaurant, the Casa Sorta, on December 1, 1982. From those overheard conversations the FBI began to understand the extent of the Mafia's hold over the construction industry in Manhattan. Langella was talking himself into a lengthy prison sentence.

THE COLOMBO FAMILY CASE

The mountain fell on Langella, Persico, and a host of other Colombo powers, on October 24, 1984. Basically, it was all over, but the crying, still formalities had to be followed.

On June 13, 1986, the fat lady had sung, and Langella was toast. Meanwhile, he had been indicted in the Commission case, so the hurts kept on coming. Once the Commission trail was over, Langella and the others were sentenced for their Colombo Family convictions. Gerry Lang was hit with a 65 year bit which meant he was going to die in prison no matter the outcome of the Commission case.

CONCLUSION

Gennaro "Gerry Lang" Langella was a very powerful Mafioso, but his strength came solely from his close connection to Carmine Persico. Without that support, Langella would most likely have fallen by the wayside. When you look back at his fate, perhaps it would have been best if he had never met Carmine Persico and instead worked at Walmart.

SALVATORE "TOM MIX" SANTORO

The life of Santoro proves that the Mafia's so-called ban on dealing in narcotics was a joke. Back in 1942, Santoro received a five-year sentence for conspiracy to import drugs from Mexico. In March of 1951, he was indicted again for conspiracy to import opium from Mexico. (It would be converted to heroin). For this crime, Santoro was given a two-year sentence.

It would have to be assumed that there were numerous times he wasn't caught during this period. It is also safe to say he didn't learn any lessons.

In 1958, Santoro was jammed up with a lot of major Mafia hoods in yet another heroin case. He was joined as a defendant by; Vito Genovese, future Genovese Family Boss Vincent "Chin" Gigante, future Bonanno Family Boss Natale Evola, and a host of other Mafiosi.

The prosecutor called Santoro, "a high overlord in the narcotics world". Santoro was sentenced to twenty years. A series of failed appeals followed, leaving Tom Mix languishing behind bars.

However, like many of his other defendants, once he was released Santoro would continue to rise through the ranks. Apparently, his attitude towards drugs changed while behind bars. On January 31, 1984, Santoro was caught on tape talking to Fat Tony Salerno about the Bonanno Family. Santoro dismissively said, "They took (inducted) too many junkies." That was like the pot calling the kettle black. (For the younger readers that's an idiom which means you are accusing someone of the same thing you do, did, or are)

UNDERBOSS

By the time Santoro was freed from his latest drug conviction, Antonio "Tony Ducks" Corallo was the power in the Lucchese Family. He quickly appointed his old friend Santoro as his Underboss. They both would remain in their respective positions through the 1986 Commission trial.

JFK AIRPORT

On February 21, 1985, the feds unveiled a 23 count racketeering indictment against Santoro, and ten other men. It was alleged that they had extorted three freight forwarding companies for a total of $350,000 in return for freedom from labor trouble. For those familiar with the excellent movie, "Goodfellas" it would be no surprise that the Lucchese Family Underboss was involved in rackets at JFK. Strike Force attorney Douglas Behm stated that the Luccheses were, "The dominant factor at the airport…"

Key to their power was their control of Teamsters Locals 295 and 851. Any freight forwarding company was at the mercy of these locals for they could threaten to call a strike for any reason thus costing the company significant money. It was simpler to pay off the union. Naturally, some of that money would go to the Lucchese leaders. Payoffs would allow a non-union company to continue operating in that cheaper manner. Trucking companies were also forced to join an association. It would also give the mobsters more control over the airport. The list of opportunities to extort money was endless. Santoro was on the receiving end of some of this cash. Fortunately for Santoro, he was eventually severed from this case.

SANTORO TALKS

Like most of the other Commission defendants, Santoro was caught on tape talking about Mafia life. On March 28, 1983, Santoro and Lucchese Capo Sal Avellino were discussing the recent appearance of former mob Boss Joe Bonanno on the "Sixty Minutes" TV show. Santoro was not a fan of Bonanno. He said, "Like he (Bonanno) says he ain't never been in narcotics, he is full of shit… they (Bonanno and Galante) were in the junk business and they were partners."

The two Lucchese mobsters continue talking about Bonanno. Santoro shed some insider light on the famous fake kidnapping pulled off by Bonanno in 1964. Santoro said, "Yeah, he kidnapped himself."

CONCLUSION

With the Commission indictment and his other legal problems, Santoro was in a world of hurt. Unfortunately for him, Tom Mix didn't have a long run at the top of the Family. He never accumulated a significant amount of money. With his advanced age and the near certainty of conviction, Santoro's life would not have a happy ending.

CHRISTOPHER "CHRISTY TRICK" FURNARI

Furnari first made the news on December 28, 1943. According to the article, he and two other mutts picked up three girls at Coney Island and drove them to some secluded spot. The lowlifes then proceeded to pound them out, presumably, because the girls were not too co-operative. Due to the fact Furnari was a second offender, he received a 15-30 year sentence. The judge commented that if one of the defendants were back in Italy, he probably wouldn't have made it to trial.

When Furnari was released in 1956, he had no trouble blending in with the Lucchese Family crew in Brooklyn. Gambling and loansharking were his staples. But he was not opposed to making money any way possible.

Furnari's real power came when he was given control of the International Brotherhood of Painters and Allied Trades District Council 9. It had approximately 6,000 painters under its umbrella. Hotels, bridges, subway stations and the like didn't get painted in NYC unless these union people did it. The possibilities for extortion, no-show jobs, loan sharking, and many other rackets were part of the deal. Furnari's hidden influence was exercised through Jim Bishop, the secretary-treasurer of the District Council.

POSITION

Furnari first appeared in the FBI files as a made member on August 1, 1963. The exact year that Furnari was elevated to Capo is elusive. He did not appear on the FBI's 1969 list of Lucchese Capos, so it had to have been after that. He was promoted to Consigliere in the early 1980s and served in that position through the 1986 Commission trial.

CONCLUSION

Furnari deliberately chose a life in LCN and rose to one of the highest positions in the Lucchese Family. He had many years of avoiding severe legal problems. It all came crashing down on his head in the 1980s.

CHAPTER TWENTY-ONE

The Commission Defendants: Part Five

ANTHONY "BRUNO" INDELICATO

Unlike the other seven defendants, Indelicato wasn't included in the Commission trial because of skills at running a racket such as loansharking or extortion. Bruno joined the others, for it was alleged he carried out three murders, at the request of the Commission. One of his victims was Carmine Galante.

THE TARGET

Carmine "Lilo" Galante was one of the most feared Mafiosi of all time. As a young adult, he was always in trouble with the police and did penitentiary time. On two occasions, he was labeled a psychopath. His most famous exploit during that era was his involvement in the assassination of the controversial writer/editor/activist, Carlo Tresca, on January 11, 1943. (Tresca had insulted the Bonanno Family Underboss, who got permission from Bonanno to whack out Tresca). There was not enough evidence to charge Galante with this hit, although he did some time on a parole violation.

By the early 1950's, Galante was in and out of Montreal, Canada, placing that wide open city's vast criminal milieu under the control of a hard-core crew of Italian Canadians. The critical racket was the Canadian's ability to obtain heroin from the chemists in Marseilles France. This put Gigante at the center of massive operation to move heroin from Europe, through Montreal, and down into New York City.

Galante started the process to become a Canadian but did not complete the journey. For many decades, writers have claimed Galante was deported from Canada. That was not the case. Events in New York required his attention, so he appointed underlings to represent him in Montreal. One of these was Phil Rastelli.

Due to the significant amount of money that Galante's Montreal operation was bringing in, he was rewarded by being appointed Underboss by Boss Joe Bonanno in 1956. This promotion would become significant years later.

In 1959, Galante's drug dealing caught up with him. He was indicted. Another case soon followed. The net result was that Galante was sentenced to 20 years on July 10, 1962. He missed the significant events of the "Banana War" described earlier in this book.

When Galante was released on January 24, 1974, the Bonanno Family leadership was still in semi-turmoil. Galante emerged from prison to find one of his former underlings, Phil Rastelli, in charge of the Family. Galante must have felt the position should have been his due to; his past service, his time spent in prison, and the fact he had been the formal Underboss.

During this period, Rastelli was severely handicapped by legal problems. He was in and out of prison then received a ten-year extortion sentence. This opened the door for Galante to seize power in the confusion.

He began inducting members and acting like the Boss. Formally, Rastelli was the Boss, but the press, the FBI, and the hoods all worked as if Galante was the head man. The Commission was soon extremely concerned about his growing power and began discussing what to do. The FBI fed into this nervousness by leaking stories to the press that Galante wanted to become the new "Boss of Bosses."

THE HIT

Bruno Indelicato was a member of a powerful crew led by his father, Alphonse "Sonny Red" Indelicato. It was this group that Consigliere Steve Cannone, picked to do the hit. Underboss Nick "Nicky Glasses" Marangello was considered too close to Galante to be included in the plotting.

Louis Giongetti rounded up the shotguns and pistols for the attack. A blue four-door Mercury Montego had been stolen earlier. It was to be used as the hit car then abandoned. Into it piled driver Santo Giordano, in the rear passenger seat was Bruno Indelicato, the other two men were Soldiers Dominick "Big Trin" Trinchera, and Russell Mauro. Backup and crash cars followed. It is safe to assume that Sonny Red was there watching over his son along with uncle J.B. Indelicato, plus a host of other Bonannos.

It was July 12, 1979. Galante was sitting on the back patio of Joe and Mary's restaurant on Knickerbocker Avenue in Brooklyn. Sitting to his right, facing the back door, was Caesar Bonventre. To Galante's left was Baldo Amato. Supposedly these two were Galante bodyguards, but they were in on the play. Seated across from Bonventre was Capo Leonard Coppola. Restaurant owner and Galante friend Giuseppe Turano was at the end of the table near Amato.

Three masked men entered the restaurant and headed for the back patio. The first was Russell Mauro, carrying a shotgun. He was followed by Bruno Indelicato, who cradled a similar weapon. Big Trin Trinchera had a pistol, which he used to gun down the restaurant owner's son when the youngster shouted a warning.

Mauro stepped onto the patio and unloaded on Galante. The veteran hood went sprawling onto his back, his cigar still in his mouth. Bonventre fired some rounds from his semi-automatic handgun into Coppola. (Casing from these shots were ejected over or through a wire fence to Bonventre's right.) Indelicato initially blasted Turano, then made sure Coppola was dead by firing two blasts into him. Bodyguard Amato was not only seen by a witness with his gun out but ballistic evidence indicted five weapons were fired thus confirming Amato was also shooting.

Outside, driver Santo Giordano was standing with his door open on the hit car. He was leaning across the roof with a rifle. The three gunmen ran out and jumped into the vehicle which roared off. It was abandoned not too far away. Meanwhile, Bonventre and Amato exited the restaurant at a fast walk. It is reasonable to assume they were picked up by a backup vehicle and taken away.

THE COMMISSION

The Commission had voted to kill Galante. Carmine Persico told his relative, Fred DeChristopher, that he cast a negative vote. If that was true, the majority must have been three to one. Gambino Boss Paul Castellano, Lucchese Boss Tony Corallo, and Genovese Boss Phil Lombardo gave their approval for the murder. Bonanno Boss Phil Rastelli was not on the Commission then. But there is no question he approved the hit.

Further evidence, of the Commission's involvement in these three murders, comes from video gathered by the NYPD, on the day of the killings. They had a camera set up across from the Ravenite Social Club on Mulberry Street in lower Manhattan. This was the headquarters of Gambino Underboss Neil Dellacroce. The cops filmed Bruno Indelicato pulling up in front of the club and receiving hugs from Bonanno Consigliere Steve Cannone and Bruno's father and uncle. Then, Cannone went into the club to presumably pass the good news on to Dellacroce. The Gambino Family was involved, for this was a Commission sanctioned hit. These murders would be a part of the Commission trial in 1986.

PROMOTION AND DISASTER

After the Galante hit, shooter Anthony "Bruno" Indelicato, and Dominick "Big Trin" Trinchera were promoted to Capo along with some other participants such as Joseph Massino, a future Boss.

Bruno was now on equal footing with his father, Sonny Red Indelicato. He was ready to make big time money. It wasn't too shocking to see Bruno, Trinchera, Phil Giacalone, and others in that alliance, attending the November 1980 wedding reception of notorious Sicilian Mafia Boss Giuseppe Bono. The festivities for the major drug dealer took place in New York at the very upscale Pierre Hotel. Indelicato's presence there was a clear indication that drugs would be a big part of his future.

The problem for the Indelicato entourage was that they needed more power to achieve their ambitions. They were being opposed by those rallying around sitting Boss Phil Rastelli such as Joey Massino and Sonny Black Napolitano. Another group was dismissively labeled, "The Zips" due to their tight connections with Sicily and their clannish behavior in the US. Major figures in this group included; Gerlando "George from Canada" Sciascia, Cesare Bonventre, and Sal Catalano. They were sitting on the fence initially but eventually joined the Rastelli forces.

THE THREE CAPOS HIT

The two rival groups danced around each other, while the Commission watched anxiously. They didn't want problems and publicity. Finally, the Rastelli group claimed to have evidence that the Indelicato crew was loading up with weapons in preparation for making a strike. Whether this was true or the Indelicatos were just getting ready to defend themselves is immaterial.

The critical thing was that the Commission gave the Rastelli group the green light to end the stalemate, by any means possible.

On May 5, 1981, Sonny Red Indelicato, Big Trin Trinchera, Phil Giacalone, and Frank Lino were lured to a Brooklyn building. They were told another peace meeting was to take place. Surprise! Surprise! Out of a closet burst Canada's Vito Rizzuto, Sal Vitale and two other hitmen from Montreal. Sonny Red, Big Trin, and Phil Lucky went down in a hail of gunfire. Even Sciascia joined in. A stunned Frank Lino burst for the door and successfully made it to safety. By most accounts, Bruno Indelicato was supposed to be present as well, but he never made it thus saving his life. The Rastelli crew were on top to stay.

CONCLUSION

Eventually, Bruno Indelicato, his uncle, and others from their crew came in from the cold and pledged allegiance to the new administration. Out of power (he had been demoted from Capo) and without his father, Indelicato then had the indignity of being indicted in the Commission case. It would not be a pleasant experience.

RALPH SCOPO

Scopo was a significant defendant during the Commission trial even though he was only a lowly Colombo Family Soldier. His power came from his position as the President and Business Manager of the Cement and Concrete Worker District Council which controlled three LIUNA locals. (Laborer's International Union). No concrete got poured in Manhattan without the co-operation of this union. That made Scopo a big man.

THE CONCRETE CLUB

This LCN racket was a no-brainer. Buildings require a foundation formed from concrete. Apartment buildings and skyscrapers not only need the concrete foundation but each floor and stairwell is constructed from the same material. Without concrete, these buildings just exist on paper. What follows is a very simplified description of the "Concrete Club".

Scopo ran the union whose members poured the concrete. The truck drivers, who brought the concrete to the job site, were members of another mobbed-up union. Having this control made it reasonably easy for the four

Mafia Families to set up a "Concrete Club." Only seven specific concrete contractors would be permitted to bid on construction jobs over $2 million. Everyone had to take their turn. The "Concrete Club" made sure the designated contractor won the job by rigging the bidding. The concrete contractor had to kick back 2% of the contract price to the "Concrete Club." From there, the money would be shared among the four Families. The Bonannos, at the time, were not members of the Commission so they did not participate in the "Concrete Club."

It all sounded straightforward, but there were endless conflicts. One of the main reasons was that all these details were kept in the heads of a variety of people. There were countless sit-downs to straighten things out. One bug caught Acting Boss Gerry Langella bitching about a decision that didn't go his way. He even threatened to shoot the other Bosses although this was just him letting off steam.

Sometimes even the heads of the four Families would have to meet to kick things back into line. On one of these occasions, the FBI was waiting outside, when the leaders and their flunkies exited a non-descript home. These pictures of the Commission members would be significant in the future. The "Concrete Club" and its operation would be the main ingredient of the Commission trial.

CONCLUSION

Scopo was a realist. On April 5, 1984, He was taped explaining the realities of his life to a contractor. Scopo told James Costigan about how the Gambino Family became concerned about one of their toughest members after he was arrested. Scopo claimed the man, Roy DeMeo, would have never talked but that didn't matter. Scopo said, "But not to take the chance (that DeMeo would talk) they went and killed him." Scopo knew the same fate might await him if things went south with the "Concrete Club".

Scopo was basically a walking dead man in the 1980s. He was pulling down a legal $305,000 from a $104,000 salary and another $201,000 in disbursements. Then were mountains of cash from all the concrete club extortions. Money wasn't the problem. It was the feds breathing down his neck. The future was not bright for Ralph Scopo.

CHAPTER TWENTY-TWO

The Good Guys

Listing all the good men and women who played a role in the decimation of the Mafia Commission circa 1986, would take far more space than this book will allow. Consequently, only profiles of some of the major characters will follow.

SENATOR ESTES KEFAUVER

Kefauver was a Senator from Kentucky who saw an opportunity to gain political advantage by latching onto a growing fear in America. By 1950, various media outlets, and crime commissions in Chicago and California had been railing against criminality. Kefauver, after a struggle, was able to obtain the necessary votes to establish the Senate Special Committee to Investigate Crime in Interstate Commerce.

Private and public hearing were held across the nation. It was not until the committee appeared in New Orleans that their work started gaining a lot of attention. In the Big Easy, a local television station gave the hearings wall to wall coverage. The response was so great that all subsequent hearings were covered. The nation was fascinated by an endless array of mobsters and crooked cops appearing on their screens. Kefauver was a star.

The Committee made a series of recommendations to fight crime. But its real importance was the fact that people began to understand that some crime was organized. Due to its link to the political process, organized crime was a danger that had to be addressed.

Kefauver parleyed his fame into two unsuccessful runs for the Democratic Party's nomination for president. He failed in 1952 but was selected as the vice presidential candidate in 1956. Kefauver and Adlai Stevenson lost to President Eisenhower.

SGT. EDGAR CROSWELL, NEW YORK STATE POLICE

It was Croswell, aided by Trooper Vincent Vasisko and Agents Ken Brown and Arthur Ruston of the Alcohol and Tax Unit of the IRS who discovered the famous 1957 National Meeting of La Cosa Nostra near Apalachin, New York. Croswell made the critical decision to set up a roadblock to identify those in attendance as they drove away. He also ordered the round-up of many hoods who tried to flee on foot. Suddenly, these characters were out of the shadows. The public and the politicians were clamoring to know why they were all gathered near this tiny hamlet.

This discovery spun off an endless series of inquiries and legal maneuvers and finally forced J. Edgar Hoover, head of the FBI, to begin serious, in-depth investigations of the leading Mafia figures. No longer would LCN be able to hide in the shadows.

The Apalachin meeting was used in the Commission case to provide proof that the Mafia and the Commission existed in the past and was not a figment of someone's imagination. The excellent police work of Croswell et al. might have been good fortune for the public, but it certainly was bad news for LCN.

SENATOR JOHN MCLELLAN

McClellan was the Democratic Senator for Arkansas from 1943 till his death in 1977. His list of accomplishments is long, but for our purposes, we will focus on his efforts against organized crime.

Beginning in January of 1957, a McClellan chaired Senate Subcommittee conducted hearings into corruption and racketeering in unions. With Robert Kennedy as the lead counsel, the committee heard testimony from a host of crooked mobsters and union officials. They also focused on the November 14, 1957, National Meeting of La Cosa Nostra and pulled many of the lead characters out from the shadows. In truth, the mob did not lose control of the Teamsters and other unions, but at least the connection between the two was out in the open for all to see.

In 1963, the so-called Valachi hearings were held. Genovese turncoat Joe Valachi was brought before the committee and a national television audience to tell the inside story of the history of the Five Families in New York. It was a sensation, but again, its primary value was the growing public awareness of the menace. This was an important stepping stone for the two main anti-organized crime accomplishment of the Senator.

With McClellan's vast knowledge and political power, the 1968 Omnibus Crime Control and Safe Streets Act was passed. Also, the 1970 Organized Crime Control Act was also put into law. As discussed earlier these acts contained the critical elements used to attack La Cosa Nostra successfully; legal electronic surveillance, the Witness Protection Act, and the RICO laws.

ROBERT BLAKEY

Blakey gained vital experience working for the Justice Department. He played an essential role in formulating the two critical Acts discussed above. But, it was in his role as a teacher and mentor, that he contributed the most towards decimating La Cosa Nostra.

While the RICO laws were on the books in 1970, they were not well understood by law enforcement and prosecutors. Veteran FBI Supervisor Jules Bonavolonta believes Blakey deserves the credit for finally focussing the FBI on the potential power of the RICO laws.

In 1980, Bonavolonta and Agent James Kossler spent three days with Blakey, learning about how to use the legal electronic surveillance and the RICO laws to conduct in-depth investigations of LCN. They hoped to use these tools to decimate the Mafia's leadership. Bonavolonta wrote that "The guy was a fucking genius."

JAMES KOSSLER

Kossler was a Marine and Vietnam War vet before his long career with the FBI. From 1976 to 1990 he led the FBI's Special Operations Division in New York. His team placed vital bugs and telephone taps in a variety of locations. Among the targets were: the home of Gambino Boss Paul Castellano, the Palma Boy's Social Club where Anthony Salerno, front Boss of the Genovese Family, held court, the Casa Sorta restaurant where Jerry Langella, the Acting Boss of the Colombo Family chowed down, and a host of other key locations. FBI Director Louis Freeh said, "He (Kossler) took the bureau sort of light years ahead of where we were at the time." Without the electronic surveillance provided by Kossler's team, the Commission case would not have been possible.

RON GOLDSTOCK

Goldstock took over the New York State Organized Crime Task Force in 1981. His team successfully bugged the vehicle in which Lucchese Boss Anthony Corallo was taxied around New York in. Corallo and driver Sal Avellino were taped talking about the Commission and the various disputes that needed to be adjudicated by that entity. Goldstock began to see the possibility of indicting the heads of the Commission all at once. He shared this evidence and his thoughts with Rudy Giuliani, the US Attorney in the Southern District. These actions would prove to be critical in the Commission case success.

RUDY GIULIANI

Giuliani was one of the key figures in the Commission case. He had spent time as an Assistant District Attorney in the Southern District before a stint as an Associate Attorney General in Washington. This gave him the practical and political experience and connections that were great assets once he was returned to the Southern District as the head man in 1983. Right away, he declared that organized crime would be his top priority. This coincided perfectly with the already on-going investigations by the FBI and the Organized Crime Task Force.

A consensus evolved that it might be possible to attack the ruling body of La Cosa Nostra, the Commission. Giuliani had the political weight to get the head honchos in Washington on board. They would provide added resources, and the muscle to pull in investigative materials gathered by a variety of authorities and jurisdictions. The Commission indictment would not have happened without him.

MICHAEL CHERTOFF

Chertoff was an Assistant US Attorney in the Southern District when Giuliani chose him to lead the prosecution team in the Commission case. He was ably assisted by John Savarese and John Childers. They had to deal with 85 witnesses, 150 tapes, and hundreds of other exhibits like surveillance photographs. Additionally, they were facing seven defendants accompanied by skilled defense lawyers except for Carmine Persico who acted as his own counsel. It was a massive undertaking, which the Chertoff team handled well.

The next chapter will describe the trial.

CHAPTER TWENTY-THREE

The Trial

Jury selection began in the much anticipated Commission trial on September 8, 1986. Eight days later, an anonymous jury of eight women and four men were seated. Six alternates were chosen the following day. The circus was ready.

THE DEFENDANT'S LAWYERS:

Anthony Cardinale for Anthony "Fat Tony" Salerno
James LaRosa for Christopher "Christy Trick" Furnari
Carmine Persico for himself, assisted by attorney Stanley Meyer
Frank Lopez for Gennaro "Gerry Lang" Langella
Sam Dawson for Salvatore "Tom Mix" Santoro
John Jacobs for Ralph Scopo
Robert Blossner for Anthony "Bruno" Indelicato
Albert Gaudelli for Anthony "Tony Ducks" Corallo

THE PROSECUTORS:

Michael Chertoff
John Savarese
J. Gilmore Childress

THE JUDGE:

Richard Owen

Note:
Corallo, Santoro, Furnari, and Scopo were free on bail during the entire trial. Persico and Langella were already incarcerated on other charges. In a controversial move, contested all the way to the Supreme Court, Salerno was denied bail under the new Bail Reform Act. The court ruled that the government's interest in protecting society trumped the individual's right to freedom.

OPENING ARGUMENTS

MICHAEL CHERTOFF

Michael Chertoff, a young Assistant United States Attorney, opened the trial. Chertoff said that the government would prove that both the Mafia and its Commission existed. The defendants, who were identified as Bosses, (Salerno, Persico, Corallo) were among the Commission members who met periodically to: settle disputes, split the money, accept new members, and sometimes approve death sentences.

He went on to explain that the other defendants were lower level members, who helped carry out the Commission's orders. He also told the jury that the government would show that the defendants used mob-controlled unions to maintain a stranglehold over the New York construction industry. Lastly, the Assistant US Attorney claimed that the Commission was responsible for the July 1979 killing of Bonanno leader, Carmine Galante and that defendant Anthony Indelicato was involved in that hit.

SAM DAWSON

Sam Dawson, Anthony "Tony Ducks" Corallo's attorney, opened for the defense. He stunned the courtroom by admitting there was a Mafia with a Commission. However, he said the only purpose of the Commission was to approve new members and to resolve disputes to prevent violence. Dawson went on to state that some of the defendants had construction interests and they met, but there was no extortion involved.

This admission that there was a Mafia and a Commission was a first. Apparently, the defendants and their attorneys had met before trial, and everyone realized that denying the existence of these entities would be impossible in the face of electronic surveillance that captured some of the defendants talking about both. The defendants reluctantly agreed to this strategy, as long as none of them had to admit the existence of the Mafia or Commission on the stand.

CARMINE PERSICO

The opening of Carmine "Junior" Persico, who was acting for himself, is worth noting. In his heavy Brooklyn accent, Persico told the jury that the witnesses the government used would include people who; committed murder, extortion, and any crime they could think of. He reminded the jury that these witnesses had contracts with the government which allowed them to avoid punishment for their own sins.

GOVERNMENT WITNESSES

Only a few government witnesses will be discussed below. In total, the feds put 85 people on the stand.

ANGELO LONARDO

Lonardo has spent a lifetime in the Cleveland Mafia. His father had been Boss of that Family but was murdered by rivals on October 13, 1927. Lonardo and others took revenge for this hit, and over the years, Lonardo moved upwards in the organization.

Lonardo acted as Underboss from 1976 to 1983 when he was convicted of drug dealing. He received a life sentence plus 105 years. It wasn't too surprising that he rolled over in October of 1983. As part of his deal, he was required to testify in the Commission case.

From his perch on the witness chair, Lonardo identified Salerno as Boss of the Genovese Family and a member of the Commission. He outlined the structure of a typical Mafia Family and the various duties of the Commission.

Lonardo also mentioned numerous old-time Mafia Bosses whom he had met over the years.

Lonardo also testified about making two trips to New York to seek the support of Salerno, and the Commission, for Cleveland's choice as a new leader of the Teamsters Union.

The prosecutors elicited testimony from Lonardo about his understanding of the 1980 murder of Philadelphia Boss Angelo Bruno. Lonardo explained that the Bruno hit was not sanctioned by the Commission. Those who carried out the plot were murdered. The purpose of this evidence was to show that the Commission had the power to order murders if its rules were violated.

In his cross-examination of Lonardo, Persico tried to denigrate his humanity and the reason behind his testimony. Persico got Lonardo to admit that he was convicted of drug dealing and received a lengthy sentence and that he was testifying to get out from under that burden. Perhaps the funniest question Persico sarcastically threw at Lonardo was, "You're eating pretty good?" Obviously, Persico was hoping the jury would be repelled by Lonardo's crimes and his cushy reward for becoming a witness.

JOE "JOE DOGS" CANTALUPO

Cantalupo was a fun loving, degenerate gambler, who was a long-time Associate of the Colombo Family. He was used as a witness for he could identify Persico and Langella as Colombo Family leaders. Joe Dogs could also recall witnessing Mafia Bosses gathering in his apartment, in 1968 or 1969, for a Commission meeting.

Persico tried to discredit Cantalupo's evidence by eliciting his testimony that Persico's brother had once given him a severe pounding for failing to repay a $10,000 loan. Persico angrily asked Cantalupo, "You was angry because you was beat up, and you was beat up because you didn't pay back the money."

Highly respected author, Selywn Rabb, in his best-selling "Five Families" book on the New York Mafia, wrote, "His (Persico's) argumentative question was a costly gaffe. The beating was over a loan-sharking debt, further illuminating Persico and his underlings as ruthless gangsters." The other defense lawyers couldn't have been pleased but probably didn't have the nerve to say so.

FRED DECHRISTOPHER

DeChristopher was related to Persico, through marriage, and had twice harbored the Colombo Boss while he was on the run. He was able to testify that Persico had told him that he was the Boss of the Colombos and Langella was his Underboss. DeChristopher also related how Persico had told him of the Commission's involvement in the murder of Bonanno power Carmine Galante, back in 1979. According to DeChristopher, Persico claimed he voted against the Galante hit. The identifications and the Galante murder stories supported the government's position that Persico and Langella were Colombo Family leaders, that there was a Commission, and it could order killings.

DeChristopher's testimony infuriated Persico. He probably felt that he had been generous to this man and his family and felt a broad sense of betrayal. Persico's cross-examination focused on demeaning DeChristopher. For example, when DeChristopher claimed he had paid for his own house, Persico sarcastically said, "You couldn't buy socks!" The courtroom erupted in laughter.

Later in the trial, Persico called DeChristopher's wife as the lone defense witness. She denied ever hearing Persico say he was the Boss of the Colombos nor did she ever hear the word Commission mentioned. Clearly, she hadn't gone into the Witness Protection Program with her husband.

JOE PISTONE

Pistone was a veteran FBI Agent who went undercover for six years and became close to two Bonanno members. Once he was removed from his role as Donnie Brasco, he began the long task of testifying in various mob trials including the Commission case.

Pistone gave a lengthy recital of his life as Brasco, but his chief purpose was the add evidence that a Commission existed and it had power. Pistone was able to do that for his two Bonanno friends had both told him about the Commission and how they were involved in the killing of Carmine Galante in 1979 and his replacement with Phil Rastelli.

JOHN TURANO and SALVATORE PARAVATI

One of the predicate acts in the list of charges was the killing of Bonanno leader Carmine Galante. To bring this hit to life for the jury the prosecutors brought in the clearly frightened son of the owner of the restaurant where the murder took place. His father was one of two other men gunned down with Galante. In fact, young John Turano was also wounded in the massacre. Turano really didn't have much to add other than describing the hit.

Paravati had the misfortune of being in Joe and Mary's Restaurant when Galante went down. Again, his role was to add color to the description of the hit. He had nothing further to add to the proceedings.

JAMES COSTIGAN and STANLEY STERNCHOS

These two concrete company owners had been active participants in the so-called "Concrete Club" that the prosecutors claimed was an illegal operation of the Commission.

Costigan and Sternchos, testified to avoid their own legal problems. They explained how the "Concrete Club" worked. As described earlier, all $2 million and over concrete contracts in Manhattan were exclusively controlled by the "Concrete Club." Representatives of the Genovese, Gambino, Lucchese, and Colombo Families made sure their leaders got a nice chunk of the 2% kickback that was required.

Control over the contractors was maintained by the fear they might have a labor dispute or the failure to deliver concrete to the construction sites. The mobsters were able to exert this pressure for they controlled the Union Local that the concrete truck drivers belonged to plus their man, Ralph Scopo, ran the powerful Cement and Concrete Workers District Council. Though this entity Scopo controlled three Laborers Union locals involving thousands of workers.

The "Concrete Club" would decide which concrete company would get a particular contract. They then arranged to rig the bids with other contractors so that the preferred choice would submit the lowest bid. The theory is that each "involved" concrete company would get their turn at the trough.

The prosecutors had lots of pictures and tapes to back up the testimony of Costigan and Sternchos. This evidence also included a conversation in which Scopo explained that if things went south, it was likely that he would be killed to keep him silent even though he was entirely loyal to the Mafia.

TAPES AND PICTURES

Corallo and Santoro were the only two defendants charged with being involved with loansharking conspiracy. According to the government, John DiLeo, a relative of Corallo, was running a loan-sharking operation on Staten

Island. The problem was that Staten Island was considered to be Gambino Family territory. The Gambinos got involved by ordering one of DiLeo's underlings to report to the Gambinos and not DiLeo. The latter complained to his Boss. A tape caught DiLeo asking Corallo to intercede with Paul Castellano, Boss of the Gambino Family.

Subsequently, Corallo ordered Santoro and Capo Sal Avellino to meet with Castellano and other Gambino members. At the sitdown it was agreed that DiLeo could continue his loan-sharking operation on Staten Island with some conditions. It had to run under the supervision of the Lucchese Family. Also, the Gambinos were to be kept informed of his activities. Surveillance pictures demonstrated that DiLeo was regularly reporting to his Lucchese superiors.

OTHER TAPE EVIDENCE

July 12, 1979

New York Police filmed Anthony Indelicato arriving at the Gambino Ravenite Social Club not long after the Galante murder. It appeared as if Indelicato was receiving congratulations. The fact he went to the Gambino club strongly suggested the hit was a multi-Family affair and thus involving the Commission.

October 7, 1984, Palma Boys Social Club

In 1984, the Buffalo Family was involved in a leadership dispute between the Todaro and Pieri families. Both groups looked to the Commission, represented by Salerno, to solve this conflict.

A bug placed in Salerno's Palma Boys Social Club captured the discussion about the Buffalo turmoil.

Ultimately, Salerno ordered John Pieri Sr. to tell rival Joe Todaro, that the "big boys" were involved now. In other words, the Commission would make the final decision. This tape supported the prosecutions argument that the Commission was real and had to approve the elevation of a new Boss.

January 31, 1984, Palma Boys Social Club

Salerno, Furnari, and Santoro were recorded trying to sort out the Commission's position on whether the leader of the Bonanno Family, Phil "Rusty" Rastelli, would be allowed to sit on the Commission. This was superior evidence that the Commission existed.

February 15, 1984, The Social Club
Christopher Furnari, Vincent "Fish Cafaro" and another man were recorded on this date. The three are involved in a confusing conversation as they tried to clarify which company got which contract. Then they tried to ensure that the contracts were evenly balanced. Each of the four Mafia Families was supposed to get an equal share. Although tough to follow, this tape was evidence that the "Concrete Club" existed and involved defendants Furnari and Persico.

FINGERPRINT EVIDENCE

A partial print was entered into evidence. It was from the hit car used in the Galante killing. Witnesses described a man exiting from that particular door and entering the restaurant. The print was from Indelicato.

TAPE OF JOE BONANNO ON THE SIXTY MINUTES TV SHOW

From 1931 Bonanno was both Boss of his own Family and a member of the Commission. He held those positions till he was ousted, by the Commission, in 1964. After a few years of futile attempts to regain his throne, Bonanno retired to Arizona.

In 1983, Bonanno published his autobiography, "Bonanno Man of Honor." He included lengthy information on the creation and operation of the Commission. Because of this, prosecutor Rudy Giuliani believed that Bonanno's testimony about the Commission would be invaluable at trial. However, by this point, Bonanno realized he was in a world of trouble both legally and with the Mafia. He resisted all efforts to co-operate.

Giuliani and Judge Richard Owen flew to Arizona to take a deposition from the supposedly ill Bonanno. Citing his health, Bonanno refused to talk. He was subsequently found guilty of civil contempt and was sentenced to prison. He would languish behind bars until he was finally released from his contempt, at the end of the Commission Trial.

Not being able to have Bonanno in person, the prosecutors played a tape of Bonanno's appearance on the popular CBS new show, "60 Minutes." The vain Bonanno was promoting his book and was questioned by veteran reporter Mike Wallace. While interesting, the tape's value was minimal. Bonanno admitted there was a Commission but vehemently denied that it would order a murder. He was lying of course.

Note:
What follows are brief summaries of the closing remarks of the prosecution and the defense attorneys. Not all defense attorneys are included.

THE PROSECUTION'S INITIAL CLOSING ARGUMENT

On November 7, 1986, prosecutor John F. Savarese stated that the Commission existed and was a Board of Directors of a huge criminal enterprise, "that has controlled the nation's organized crime since the 1930s." This, of course, was a vast exaggeration for there was plenty of organized crime outside the milieu of La Cosa Nostra.

Savarese went on to state that the Commission controlled the NY construction industry by forming a "Concrete Club" which handed out major concrete contracts. Also, the club extorted kickbacks of 2%. Defendant Ralph Scopo collected these payoffs for the Commission.

To counter Persico's claim that he was not on surveillance pictures of audio tapes Savarese proclaimed that Persico was Boss whether he was in or out of prison. He said that Persico used the phone and messengers to maintain control of his Family.

DEFENDANT'S CLOSING ARGUMENTS

ROBERT BLOSSNER for ANTHONY "BRUNO" INDELICATO

Indelicato was charged with the murders of Carmen Galante, and two Associates on behalf of the Commission. For Blossner, "the government's case can't stand the test of hard facts. The government wants you to guess the young man into a conviction."

ALBERT GAUDELLI for ANTHONY "TONY DUCKS" CORALLO

Gaudelli didn't play nice for he called the prosecution's case "garbage." He also took a shot at the "victims" of the "Concrete Club." "Every time they took a job they took it with the full knowledge and understanding they were to add 2%. Ladies and gentlemen, this is not extortion."

Gaudelli also sarcastically complained about law enforcement's surveillance of his client Corallo. "He couldn't get any more heat. He was in the oven. They were up his nose."

The attorney was emphatic that membership in the Mafia or the Commission was not a crime. Then he stated, "He's (Corallo) not guilty of any wrongdoing in this case."

JAMES LAROSA for CHRISTOPHER "CHRISTY TRICK" FURNARI

LaRosa made a good case for the innocence of his client. Surveillance, over a five year period, only showed Furnari meeting with other defendants four times. He was not seen with concrete contractors. LaRosa forcefully stated, "Did he put a gun to anyone's head? Show me where." He also added, "You've got to make it up if you convict him."

JOHN JACOBS for RALPH SCOPO

Jacobs had a near impossible task for not only did two witnesses testify against his client but there were reams of tapes capturing Scopo discussing the concrete industry. Nevertheless, Jacobs soldiered on admitting that Scopo had acted illegally and had taken payments but he was not charged with those offenses. Nor were his actions on behalf of the Commission. Jacobs stated, "Price fixing and bid rigging is not racketeering, not extortion either."

ANTHONY CARDINALE for ANTHONY "FAT TONY" SALERNO

Cardinale told the jury that all the government's evidence about the Commission was an effort to, "inflame you and prejudice you." He went on the claim that all the contractors were the members of the "Concrete Club" not the Commission members. He also stated that the Commission members had nothing to do with the concrete payments. "The contractors gladly paid to get an advantage" concluded Cardinale.

FRANK LOPEZ for GENNARO "GERRY LANG" LANGELLA

Lopez continued the defense strategy of claiming that the contractors were the guilty party in this case, not the defendants. He said the contractors were greedy insiders—not victims. If the jury found that the contractors were insiders, they had to find the defendants not guilty.

CARMINE PERSICO for HIMSELF

"Mafia, Mafia, Mafia! Take that out of the trial, and there is no trial." Persico forcibly proclaimed. The crime Boss emphasized that he was not seen nor heard on any of the government's vast collection of surveillance material.

Admitting that he had spent 14 years in prison on a hijacking conviction, Persico played the victim and plaintively asked, "How long do they want me to keep paying for that mistake?" "They can't send me back to jail because I was in jail. They have to prove I did something else" Persico told the jury.

Talking in the third person, Persico suggested that he might have had enough of Mafia life and thus wasn't involved in the Commission case charges. It was a very interesting and entertaining 90-minute closing.

THE PROSECUTION'S FINAL CLOSING ARGUMENT

MICHAEL CHERTOFF

Lead prosecutor Michael Chertoff finished up for the government. He called the Commission members "puppet masters." Contrary to what Persico had said in his closing, Chertoff stated, "The Mafia is very relevant to this case because it is the Mafia that makes possible this kind of concerted criminal activity." To counter the defense claim that the contractors were the instigators of the illegalities, Chertoff stated that the owners paid because of fear.

THE JUDGE'S CHARGE TO THE JURY

Judge Richard Owen spoke for about three hours on November 14, 1986. Basically, he told the 12 jurors that they had to decide whether the Mafia and the Commission existed and whether the defendants conducted its affairs in a pattern consisting of at least two racketeering acts. He then gave the case to the anonymous jury.

THE VERDICT

On November 19, 1986, the jury returned. It was a slam dunk for the prosecution.

All the defendants, except Indelicato, were convicted of one extortion conspiracy, twelve counts of extortion or attempted extortion, plus six labor bribery violations. Indelicato was convicted of the three predicate murders.

Corallo and Santoro were also convicted of the loansharking conspiracy charge.

These same convictions were then used to prove that there was a pattern of crimes committed by each defendant. When under the RICO umbrella these crimes are called "predicate acts." At least two predicate acts, within ten years of each other are required. The government easily exceeded that threshold for each defendant.

With the requirements having been met, all the defendants were convicted of both RICO Conspiracy and substantive RICO.

THE SENTENCING

On January 13, 1987, Judge Richard Owen told the courtroom that his sentences were to send a message, "To those out there who are undoubtedly thinking about taking over the reins of power." As he sentenced Salerno, the judge stated that his comments applied to all the defendants. He said, "You, sir, in my opinion, essentially spent all your lifetime terrorizing this community for your financial gain. Then the boom was lowered on each defendant individually.

Salerno: 100 years, $240,000

Persico: 100 years, $240,000

Corallo: 100 years, $250,000 (The extra $10,000 was for loan sharking)

Langella: 100 years, $240,000

Furnari: 100 years, $240,000

Santoro: 100 years, $250,000 (the extra $10,000 was for loan sharking)

Scopo: 100 years, $240,000

Indelicato: 40 years, $50,000 (20 years for RICO conspiracy and 20 years for substantive RICO)

Judge Owen immediately revoked the bail of; Corallo, Santoro, Furnari, Indelicato, and Scopo. Langella, Persico, and Salerno were in prison throughout the trial.

Note: The 100 years is actually five consecutive 20-year terms.

Note: These sentences were applied before the end of federal parole thus these men were eligible for parole.

Note: Judge Owen recommended no parole

CHAPTER TWENTY-FOUR

The Aftermath: Part One

Life went on after the defendants received their severe sentences in January 1987. What follows is a summary of their futures after this ruling.

ANTHONY "FAT TONY" SALERNO

January 15, 1987
A superseding indictment was announced accusing Salerno and others of running the Genovese Family as a Criminal Enterprise. A host of charges were laid.

April 1988
Former Salerno protégé, Vincent "Fish" Cafaro, testified before Congress that Salerno had never been the formal Boss of the Genovese Family but was a "Front Boss" for the real power, Phil "Cockeyed Phil" Lombardo.

May 4, 1988
Salerno and others were convicted in the Genovese Family trial. However, he was found not guilty of rigging the Teamsters leadership election and the murder of Philadelphia Capo John

Simone. The latter was involved in the killing of Philadelphia Boss Angelo Bruno in 1980. Eventually, Salerno received 70 years.

January 1989
The Second Circuit Court of Appeals affirmed Salerno's Commission convictions and sentence.

April 8, 1989
Salerno pleaded guilty to a Genovese Family racketeering case in New Jersey.

September 7, 1989
Salerno was sentenced to five years for his New Jersey conviction.

October 1989
The Supreme Court confirmed Salerno's convictions in the Commission case.

June 28, 1991
The Second Circuit Court of Appeals reversed the convictions of Salerno and others from May 4, 1988. It ruled that the District Court Judge should have admitted the exculpatory grand jury evidence of two men.

June 1992
The Supreme Court remanded the ruling back to the Second Circuit.

July 27, 1992
Salerno died at the Medical Center for Federal Prisoners in Springfield, Missouri. He has been there since 1989. He was stricken with a stroke and died about a week later.

August 17, 1992
The Second Circuit Court of Appeals again reversed the convictions of Salerno's co-defendants from May 4, 1988. Salerno's appeal was dismissed because he had died.

ANTHONY "TONY DUCKS" CORALLO

Corallo went quietly into the night. He did not face any further trials and arranged an orderly transfer of power.

November 19, 1986
At a meeting, Corallo designated Victor Amuso as Acting Boss, Neil Migliore as Acting Underboss, and Anthony "Gaspipe" Casso as Acting Consigliere. All three would have their positions become formal after the sentencing of Corallo, Santoro, and Furnari in January of 1987.

January 1989
The Second Circuit Court of Appeals affirmed Corallo's convictions and sentence in the Commission trial.

October 1989
The Supreme Court affirmed Corallo's convictions in the Commission case

August 23, 2000
Corallo died at the Medical Center for Federal Prisoners at Springfield, Missouri. Prosecutor Michael Chertoff reflected that "He was very passive in court. He sat there like one of these big stone idols." An anonymous friend said this about Corallo. "He enjoyed pasta, opera, and working in his garden. He cherished his privacy and his family was the dearest thing to him in the world."

SALVATORE "TOM MIX" SANTORO

After being involved in the discussions with Corallo and Furnari over the appointments of replacements for them all, Santoro basically faded from history.

January 1989
The Second Circuit Court of Appeals affirmed Santoro's convictions and sentence in the Commission trial.

October 1989
The Supreme Court affirmed Santoro's convictions in the Commission case.

January 2000
Santoro passed away in the Medical Center for Federal Prisoners in Springfield, Missouri

GENNARO "GERRY LANG" LANGELLA

Before the verdict in the Commission case, Langella was sentenced to 65 years for his conviction in the Colombo Family trial in June 1986.

Langella had been demoted from his Underboss, and Acting Boss roles after his arrest in 1984. He was replaced by Persico's cousin, Andy Russo.

January 1989
The Second Circuit Court of Appeals affirmed Langella's convictions and sentence in the Commission trial.

October 1989
The Supreme Court affirmed Langella's conviction in the Commission case.

December 15, 2013
Langella died in the Medical Center for Federal Prisoners in Springfield, Missouri. In his obituary, in the Staten Island Advance, his niece Donna wrote, "He was very good-hearted, generous, and helpful to family and friends... he enjoyed playing cards and spending time with his family." Noted author Selwyn Raab had a different take on Langella. "...he was a ruthless, arrogant loan shark and drug trafficker" commented Raab.

RALPH SCOPO

Scopo went quietly off to prison with his power entirely gone. Perhaps he had some money left after lawyer fees and legal fines. Fortunately for him, Scopo did not live to see the misfortune of his two sons who remained in the milieu of La Cosa Nostra.

January 1989
The Second Circuit Court of Appeals affirmed Scopo's convictions
and sentence in the Commission trial.

October 1989
The Supreme Court affirmed Scopo's conviction in the
Commission case.

March 9, 1993
Scopo died in Lewisburg prison.

March 18, 1987
The feds launched a Civil RICO case against the Colombo Family.
One of the results was that Scopo's son Ralph was banned from
Local 6A of the Laborer's Union and also from the Cement and
Concrete District Council. These were the former strongholds of
Ralph Scopo Sr.

Oct 20, 1993
Scopo's son Joe aligned himself with the Victor Orena faction
which was trying to wrestle control of the Colombo Family from
the Persico crew. He became Orena's Underboss but was gunned
down on this date.

ANTHONY INDELICATO

For a brief time, Indelicato's luck seemed to change.

January 31, 1989
All the defendants appealed to the Second Circuit Court of
Appeals about their convictions and sentences. Only Indelicato
won a partial victory

Indelicato had been convicted of RICO conspiracy and substantive
RICO. The jury had been convinced that he had been a participant
in the 1979 murders of Bonanno power Carmine Galante and two
of his Associates on behalf of the Commission.

The judges of the Second Circuit eventually decided that while Indelicato's RICO conspiracy could stand, the substantive RICO conviction had to be reversed. They ruled that the killings did not meet a required timeline.

Indelicato's sentences had been 20 years for the RICO conspiracy count and another 20 years for the substantive RICO conviction. Now, he was facing a 20-year hill to climb rather than 40 years. In turn, this meant he would be eligible for parole much earlier.

October 1989
Indelicato had argued through the appeals courts that the government had not proven he had committed the required, "pattern of racketeering" that is a necessary element of a RICO conspiracy conviction. Briefly, he claimed that the three 1979 murders he committed on behalf of the Commission were, in fact, one predicate act not the required two. His lawyer also argued that there was a time problem with the convictions. The Supreme Court ruled against Indelicato leaving him still facing the 20 years on the RICO conspiracy conviction.

2000
Indelicato was released on parole from his Commission sentence. He had done 13 years.

February 14, 2001
Indelicato drove the hit car in the murder of mob associate Frank Santoro. Acting Bonanno Boss, Vinny "Vinny Gorgeous" Basciano had ordered the death because he believed Santoro had threatened to kidnap his kids.

November 19, 2004
Indelicato was among a group of mobster indicted on various charges including the 2001 Santoro murder.

August 6, 2008
Indelicato pled out to the Santoro murder.

December 16, 2008
Indelicato was sentenced to 20 years for the Santoro killing. His projected release date is September 28, 2023. He will be 76. Indelicato is currently at the federal prison in Danbury, Connecticut.

CHRISTOPHER FURNARI

January 1989
The Second Circuit Court of Appeals affirmed Furnari's convictions and sentence in the Commission trial.

October 1989
The Supreme Court upheld Furnari's Commission sentence.

December 1996
Furnari was up for his first parole hearing. The government argued that Furnari had committed murders and other violent acts during his life. Using this information the Parole Commission gave Furnari a Category Eight rating. That is the worst rating possible and meant he would probably never be granted parole. Also, the Parole Commission set his next parole hearing for 2011.

Furnari had to have been devastated for he was not charged with any murders or violence in the Commission case. He then launched into 18 years of grinding, frustrating, costly and seemingly endless litigation hoping to win his freedom.

In very simple terms Furnari felt he had been unfairly labeled a violent criminal. Furthermore, he believed that Parole Commission's conclusion relied too heavily on questionable information provided by controversial turncoat Anthony "Gaspipe" Casso. His arguments never worked. Furnari remained in prison till 2014.

September 19, 2014
After a parole hearing, Furnari was released from a prison hospital in Minnesota. He was 90. By this time he was extremely ill.

May 28, 2018
Furnari passed away in his home. In his obituary, he was described as a "Loving husband, father, and grandfather, and friend to many."

CARMINE PERSICO

After being on the run for a period of time, Persico was arrested on February 15, 1985. He has been behind bars ever since. Unbelievably he has managed to remain the Boss of the Family to the present day. (2018)

January 1989
The Second Circuit Court of Appeals affirmed Persico's convictions and sentence in the Commission trial.

October 1989
The Supreme Court upheld Persico's convictions and 100-year sentence.

1991
Persico moved to vacate his 1986 Commission sentence, but trial Judge Richard Owen denied this motion.

1991
The Second Circuit Court of Appeals affirmed Judge Owen's decision to deny Persico's motion to vacate.

June 24, 2016
An order was entered by the US District Court for the South District of New York denying Persico's motion to correct his sentence.

April 21, 2017
The Second Circuit Court of Appeals affirmed the order of the District Court on June 24, 2016. It also rejected all Persico's claims of government wrongdoing at his trial and sentencing.

At present (2018) it looks as if Persico will die in prison.

CHAPTER TWENTY-FIVE

The Aftermath: Part Two

REACTION TO THE COMMISSION CASE VICTORY

The reaction to the government victory in the Commission case was almost entirely positive, as the following examples demonstrate.

William Doran, Chief of the FBI's criminal division in New York commented, "This will have a tremendous impact on the Mafia. It will cause turmoil in the ranks and smooth the way for future undercover operations."

The convictions will help destroy, "The myth that the leadership of the Mafia is untouchable," said Assistant US District Attorney Dennison Young.

Rudy Giuliani was quoted as saying that the convictions, "Will result in dismantling the ruling Commission of La Cosa Nostra."

For Thomas L. Sheer, the director of the FBI inspection division, "A lot of (criminal) networks are going to crumble."

A headline in the New York Times on November 20, 1986, read, "Landmark verdict could disrupt the mob."

Ronald Goldstock, Director of the New York State Organized Crime Task Force, commented, "...mobsters in a position to seek top roles are preferring to stay in the background. They recognize that the new leadership will be immediately targeted..."

EFFECT ON THE COMMISSION

The Commission was formed, in 1931, at a National Meeting of the leaders of the approximately 26 La Cosa Nostra Families. The Bosses decided future National Meetings would be held every five years. The primary purpose would be to select the seven man membership of the Commission. In effect, the Commission members would be serving five-year terms. National Meetings were held in; 1931, 1936, 1941, 1946, 1951, and 1956.

In November of 1957, an out of sequence, emergency National Meeting of La Cosa Nostra was discovered at Apalachin, New York. As described earlier in this book, the resulting publicity led to many grand juries, public hearings, deportation attempts, court cases, and the like. It was a total disaster for La Cosa Nostra. It was the last National Meeting ever held.

The membership of the Commission was no longer determined by a vote at a National Meeting. The sitting Commission members rubber-stamped their next five-year term. In time, the five-year term disappeared. A Boss sat on the Commission in perpetuity. Only death, natural or violent, or an extremely lengthy prison term, created a change. Joe Bonanno was an exception in that he was deposed as Boss of the Bonanno Family thus also losing his Commission seat. He went off into retirement in Arizona.

NO MORE COMMISSION?

The Commission convictions in 1986 had a similar effect as Apalachin. For all intents and purposes, formal meetings of the Bosses of the five New York Families were over. It was far too dangerous for the leaders to gather. Discovery was a very likely possibility. Thomas Reppetto, author of "American Mafia," was quoted as saying, "Today it is too dangerous for it to meet."

JOEY MASSINO

Joe Massino, Boss of the Bonanno Family from 1991 until he became a turncoat in 2004, confirmed this assessment. When he testified at the 2011 murder trial of Bonanno Acting Boss Vincent "Vinny Gorgeous" Basciano, Massino said, "There ain't no Commission. When Paul Castellano got killed in December of 1985, there was never another Commission meeting there."

THE COMMISSION LIVES ON

But Massino's assessment is contradicted by the information provided by turncoat Gambino Family Underboss Sam "Sammy the Bull" Gravano. He claimed that Gotti called a meeting of the Commission in 1988. Gravano set up the gathering along with the Genovese Underboss, Vincent Mangano, and Lucchese Consigliere Anthony Casso.

Gotti (Gambino Family), Vincent "Chin" Gigante (Genovese Family), and Vic Amuso (Lucchese Family) met in an apartment. The Dapper Don urged that Carmine Persico's Acting Boss, Vic Orena, should have a seat for the Colombo Family. That was agreed to.

Then Gotti pushed to have the Bonanno Family regain their Commission spot. Gotti's friend Joe Massino sat on the Bonanno throne at this time. If he were brought into the meetings, Gotti figured he would control the Commission. He would have three out of the five votes. (Gambino, Colombo, and Bonanno)

Gigante was no fool and quickly recognized what Gotti was attempting to accomplish. Accordingly, he said that the Bonanno question would have to be resolved at the next Commission meeting. He was supported by the Lucchese Family thus winning the vote two to one. The Bonannos were still on the outside.

RALPH NATALE

One time Philadelphia Boss, Ralph Natale, gave us some insight into whether the Commission was functioning after 1986.

Natale's claim to be a member of La Cosa Nostra, let alone a Boss, is very questionable. Most accounts have Natale being made by renegade Philadelphia soldier Joey Merlino. There is no evidence that this induction was approved by the Commission. Nor was there any recognized Philadelphia Family administration member present at the ceremony.

At the time John Stanfa was the Boss, but his credentials were also suspect. Merlino and Natale had been plotting for some time to gain control of the Family. Technically, Natale's induction was entirely invalid.

Years later, in his biography, "The Last Don Standing" Natale attempted to counter this accusation by claiming he had been formally made, in 1966, in a secret ceremony by Gambino Boss Carlo Gambino and Philadelphia Boss Angelo Bruno.

No one took this ludicrous account seriously. For one thing, why would Natale let Merlino conduct an induction ceremony if he was already made?

Secondly, why wouldn't he have already told his minions that he was a formal member thus strengthening his right to attempt to become Boss? The answer is simple. Natale was most likely lying about his 1966 induction.

Despite this questionable legitimacy, Natale's writing sheds some light as to whether the Commission was operating after 1986. When trying to bring Joey Merlino and Michael Ciancaglini into his vision of taking over the Philadelphia Family, Natale brought up the Commission. In his book, Natale claimed he said, "It is important that I show real strength from here in prison, so when the time comes, the Commission will recognize us." Whether accurate or not, in 1990, Natale believed the Commission was a functioning body.

JOEY MASSINO 2

In his 2011 court testimony, Massino stated that the Commission no longer existed. Then he contradicted himself. Massino described a meeting he called of the leaders of the five New York Families. Five people showed up. Only one was a formal Boss. That was Massino himself.

Massino named the other four Family representative who were present as; Acting Boss Louis "Louie Bagels" Daidone of the Lucchese Family, Acting Boss Joel "Joe Waverley" Cacace of the Colombo Family, Acting Boss Peter Gotti of the Gambino Family, and Lawrence "Skinny Larry" Dentico of the Genovese Family.

For Massino, this bunch of characters was a far cry from the days when the Commission meetings were attended by all five Bosses. But it was still a formal Commission meeting in my opinion.

THE GOTTIS

Two incidents, involving John Gotti and his son, suggest that the Commission continued operating after 1986. On October 25, 1996, the New York Times reported that the Genovese, Lucchese, Colombo, and Bonanno Families had ordered Gotti to step down as Boss of the Gambino Family. At the time Gotti was in prison. The Times said that this statement was based on information gathered from informers and wiretaps by Federal prosecutors and investigators.

The second example came from a February 3, 1997, federal raid on a business controlled by John Gotti Jr. They discovered a series of induction lists. That was a first. The Five Families were still circulating the names of potential inductees. The Commission seemed to be still approving new members.

THE GOOD GUYS SPEAK

DANIEL CASTLEMAN

Castleman was the Manhattan District Attorney's chief of investigations when he made these comments in 1998. He stated, "it's too early to tell if the Commission is permanently dead. But without a Commission, there will be a significant disruption in the ability of organized crime… to make a comeback in the industries, they once dominated."

BRUCE MOUW

The former FBI Agent said, "They are talking Capo to Capo and Soldier to Soldier. A lot of issues and beefs between the Families now stay up in the air for years."

WHY DIDN'T THE COMMISSION MEET

Most accounts report that the Commission was not meeting due to the turmoil in the leadership of the Gambino, Lucchese and Colombo Families. For the more stable Bonanno and Genovese Families, meeting with the others brought the increased possibility of leaks and discovery. It just wasn't worth it. The fact there were no common rackets such as the "Concrete Club" and the garbage industry were further reasons to avoid meeting.

CONCLUSION

There were really three versions of the Commission. They are each briefly outlined below.

COMMISSION 1

It was inaugurated, in 1931, and ran without interruption till 1957. Its membership was formally elected by all the Bosses of the 26 some La Cosa Nostra Families. This version of the Board of Directors had huge prestige and power.

COMMISSION 2

After the 1957 fiasco at Apalachin, New York, it was no longer possible for all the Mafia Bosses to meet every five years to give their blessing to the membership of the Commission. The members simply ratified themselves. Nevertheless, the body still held great power and prestige although it was fraying at the edges as demonstrated by their inability to end the Gallo and Banana Wars quickly. The 1986 Commission convictions brought this version of the Commission to a slow end.

COMMISSION 3

As the 21st Century began, the days of all five New York Family Bosses regularly meeting was over. The Commission continued to exist in name, but in reality, the process was now minimal meetings between lower-ranking members when an interfamily dispute arose. The Commission was but a shadow of itself.

CONCLUSION

The world of La Cosa Nostra would be unrecognizable to the first seven Commission members.

Families have disappeared in; Buffalo, Denver, Dallas, Kansas City, Los Angeles, Madison WI, Milwaukee, New Orleans, Pittsburgh Pittston Pa., Rochester, San Francisco, Springfield Ill, San Jose, St. Louis, and Tampa. Some of these cities have a few made guys walking (or limping) around, but these would not be legitimately called Families.

Shaky regimes still plug along in Philadelphia, New England, and New Jersey. The Chicago Outfit, although much reduced in size, soldiers on with a firm structure in place. It also appears that the Detroit Family is still in existence but keeps a very low profile. Their days of great power when they controlled serious parts of the Teamsters and had a seat on the Commission are long gone.

While under nearly relentless siege by the good guys, the five New York Families have managed to survive with firm structures in place. Changes happen regularly, but they still manage to get someone to take over leadership on either a temporary or permanent basis.

The original form of the Commission is long gone. So too is its second version which was virtually ended in 1986. The present edition might still be called the Commission by some, but it is certain that Bonanno, Profaci, Gagliano, Magaddino, Capone, Profaci, and Mangano, the original members, would be entirely dismissive of its credibility.

APPENDIX A

Commission Membership 1931-1957

YEAR	FAMILY	NAME	REPLACED	REASON
1931	Bonanno	Joe Bonanno		
1931	Buffalo	Stefano Magaddino		
1931	Chicago	Al Capone		
1931	Colombo	Joe Profaci		
1931	Gambino	Vince Mangano		
1931	Genovese	Lucky Luciano		
1931	Lucchese	Tommaso Gagliano		
1932	Chicago	Frank Nitti	Al Capone	In prison
1937	Genovese	Frank Costello	Lucky Luciano	In prison
1943	Chicago	Paul Ricca	Frank Nitti	Suicide
1947	Chicago	Tony Accardo	Paul Ricca	In prison
1951	Lucchese	Tom Lucchese	Tommaso Gagliano	Died
1957	Chicago	Sam Giancanna	Tony Accardo	Stepped down
1957	Genovese	Vito Genovese	Frank Costello	Retired under pressure
1957	Gambino	Carlo Gambino	Albert Anastasia	Killed

Beginning in 1931, a National Meeting of La Cosa Nostra was held every five years. At these gatherings the membership of the Commission would be ratified by a vote of all the LCN Bosses in the USA. The discovery of the 1957 National Meeting ended this practice.

APPENDIX B

Commission Membership 1958-1986

YEAR	FAMILY	NAME	REPLACED	REASON
1958	Bonanno	Joe Bonanno		
1958	Buffalo	Stefano Magaddino		
1958	Chicago	Sam Giancanna		
1958	Colombo	Joe Profaci		
1958	Gambino	Carlo Gambino		
1958	Genovese	Vito Genovese		
1958	Lucchese	Tom Lucchese		
1961	Detroit	Joe Zerilli		New Member
1961	Philadelphia	Angelo Bruno		New Member
1964	Bonanno	Gaspar DiGregorio	Joe Bonanno	Deposed
1964	Colombo	Joe Colombo	Joe Profaci	Died 1962
1966	Bonanno	Paul Sciacca	Gaspar DiGregorio	Stepped down
1967	Chicago	Sam Battaglia	Sam Giancanna	In prison

1967	Lucchese	Carmine Tramunti	Tom Lucchese	Died
1967	Genovese	Phil Lombardo	Vito Genovese	Stepped down while in prison
1968	Lucchese	Tony Corallo	Carmine Tramunti	In prison
1968	Chicago	Phil Alderisio	Sam Battaglia	In prison
1969	Chicago	Jackie Cerone	Phil Alderisio	In prison
1970	Bonanno	Natale Evola	Paul Sciacca	Retired due to legal problems and ill health
1971	Chicago	Joey Aiuppa	Jackie Cerone	In prison
1971	Colombo	Carmine Persico	Joe Colombo	Shot and incapacitated
1973	Bonanno	Phil Rastelli	Natale Evola	Died
1974	Buffalo	Lost its seat	Stefano Magaddino	Died
1976	Gambino	Paul Castellano	Carlo Gambino	Died
1976	Bonanno	Membership suspended	Phil Rastelli	Turmoil and drug dealing in the Family
1977	Detroit	Lost its seat	Joe Zerilli	Died
1980	Philadelphia	Lost its seat	Angelo Bruno	Killed
1981	Genovese	Vincent Gigante	Phil Lombardo	Forced retirement
1985	Gambino	John Gotti	Paul Castellano	Killed

The convictions in the 1986 Commission Case ended the practice of the Bosses of the Five Families meeting together. Fear of discovery was the main reason for this decision.

Note:
Carmine Persico was not "officially" the Colombo Boss till 1980. Tom DiBella was "officially" the Boss from 1973 to 1980. However, everyone knew Persico was the real Boss. That is why his Commission seat is listed as starting in 1971, the year Colombo was incapacitated.

APPENDIX C

Commission Membership 1987-2018

During this era, the five Bosses of the New York Families never met as the Commission. It was impossible since Carmine Persico of the Colombos was locked up. Also, no one wanted to take the chance of being discovered together by the good guys. The Families would still meet, but it was usually in twos or threes. Most often it was someone representing the Boss who was present.

Note:
The following chart only lists the formal Bosses who theoretically sat on the Commission. Some of these men were in prison during most of the "membership."

The Chicago Outfit is not included. After the 1957 Apalachin disaster, their Boss was more and more reluctant to get involved with New York Mafia politics. As the mobs hold on big international unions faded in the 80s and 90s, there really was no reason for the Chicago Outfit to be a formal member of the Commission.

YEAR	FAMILY	NAME	REPLACED	REASON
1987	Colombo	Carmine Persico		In prison
1987	Gambino	John Gotti		
1987	Genovese	Vincent Gigante		
1987	Lucchese	Vic Amuso	Anthony Corallo	In prison
1991	Bonanno	Joe Massino		Family returned to the Commission
2002	Gambino	Peter Gotti	John Gotti	Died in prison
2004	Bonanno	Various Acting Bosses	Joe Massino	Became a government witness
2005	Genovese	Various Acting Bosses	Vincent Gigante	Died in prison
2011	Gambino	Domenico Cefalu	Peter Gotti	In Prison
2013	Bonanno	Mike Mancuso	Various Acting Bosses	Mancuso became the first official Boss since Massino became a government witness.
2015	Gambino	Frank Cali	Domenico Cefalu	Retired
2015	Genovese	Liborio Bellomo	Various Acting Bosses	Bellomo became the first formal Genovese Boss since 2005. The date of 2015 is approximate.

Printed in April 2022
by Rotomail Italia S.p.A., Vignate (MI) - Italy